W9-AWO-956

A CONCISE DICTIONARY OF INTERIOR DESIGN

Frederic H. Jones, Ph.D

CRISP PUBLICATIONS, INC.
Los Altos, California

A CONCISE DICTIONARY OF INTERIOR DESIGN

Frederic H. Jones, Ph.D

CREDITS
Editor in Chief: **Frederic H. Jones, Ph.D**
Associate Editor: **Regina Sandoval**
Contributing Editors: **Linda Sandoval**
Judith Jones
William J. Fielder

Copyright © 1990 by Frederic H. Jones, Ph.D
Printed in the United States of America

Library of Congress Catalog Card Number 91-70348
Jones, Frederic H., Ph.D
A Concise Dictionary of Interior Design
ISBN 1-56052-067-1

70885

INTRODUCTION

Concise Dictionary of Interior Design

This project has truly been a labor of love. Words have been a fascination for me all my life. I have collections of dictionaries, glossaries, word lists, etc. in many languages and on many subjects. I suppose it was just a matter of time before I was compelled to undertake a word list project of my own. I hope you find it both interesting and useful.

Many of the words and definitions included here were provided by historic dictionaries of architecture and design including the late 19th century edition by Russell Sturgis. Many of the illustrations have also been derived from these sources. In all cases the language and definitions were updated when necessary. Another primary source of words and their definitions were various associations and trade organizations. They include: The Illumination Engineering Society, Carpet and Rug Institute, Western Institute of Cabinetmakers, and many others. I wish to acknowledge their invaluable assistance and hasten to add that errors, no doubt, derive from my translation rather than from their creation.

My hope is that this and the other dictionaries in the series serve as introductory aids to students of design and architecture. The need to know both the meaning of obscure words and the obscure meanings of familiar words is one that a student of any profession encounters early in their studies. In fact the very "putting on of the mantle" of the language of the profession is the very essence of engaging the profession. We find ourselves sounding and thinking like designers and eventually we become the thing we emulate. This list of words will serve as an incomplete but helpful map on this journey.

I, in the process of editing this dictionary encountered many words and illustrations that would extend beyond the scope of any single dictionary. I have also been very involved in the contemporary process of automating the very word management and drawing management tools essential to design practice. I speak of the computer of course. I therefore have combined the extensive database of words and images and the computer and am making available an electronic "encyclopedia" of architecture and design. If you are interested in this product please contact me at 39315 Zacate Avenue, Fremont, CA 94538.

Frederic H. Jones, Ph.D

A

"A" size sheet: 8 1/2" x 11"

A.C.: Alternating current.

Aaron's rod: An ornament consisting of a straight molding of rounded section, with leafage or scroll work seeming to emerge from it.

Abated: In stone cutting, hammered metal work, and the like, cut away or beaten down, lowered in any way, as the background of a piece of ornament, so as to show a pattern or figure in relief.

Abat-jour: In French, anything which serves to throw daylight or other light downward, or in a given direction; from the movable shade of a lamp to the sloping soffit of a window.

Abat-sons: In French, anything intended to reflect sound, as of a bell, downward or horizontally.

Abat-voix: In French, a sounding board.

Abrasion resistance: A material's ability to resist rubbing and scraping.

Absorbent powder: A commercially prepared powder of granulated corn cobs, or sawdust, or any other suitable carrier, containing a detergent and a dry solvent.

Absorbents: Sound absorbing materials.

Abstract art: Art that is not representative or naturalistic in design.

Abut: To touch, or join, by its end; as in a timber where the end grain is planted against another member of a structure, but without framing; or where an arch bears upon a pier, course of stone, skew back, or the like.

Acajou: (French) Mahogany.

ACANTHUS, NATURAL.
From drawing by John Ruskin.

Acanthus: (A) A plant growing freely in the lands of the

Mediterranean, having large leaves, deeply cleft; the sharp pointed leaves of some species strongly resembling those of the familiar field and roadside thistles, Carduus (or Cnicus, Gray) Lanceolatus, Virginianus, and others. The two species commonly described and figured, Acanthus mollis and A. spinosus, are very different in the character of the leaves. (B) In Greek, Greco-Roman, Byzantine, Romanesque, and neoclassic architecture, a king of decorative leafage, assumed to be studied, or to have been studied originally from the plant.

Acatia: A dense wood, resembling rosewood, used in making furniture with turned parts and handles. It is yellowish-red to reddish-brown in color and is native primarily to Australia.

Accent color: Enhance the decoration by using, in moderate quantities, an intense color to differentiate a scheme.

Accent lighting: Directional lighting to emphasize a particular object or to draw attention to a part of the field of view.

Accessible: A means of approach, admittance and use, for use by physically handicapped people.

Accessories: Decorative items that convey personality and offer charm to a room and declare a person's individuality. See bibelot.

Accolade: An ornamental treatment of the archivolt or hood molding of an arch or of the moldings of an apparent arch, or of a form resembling an arch, as in late Gothic work; consisting of a reverse curve tangent on either side to the curves of the arch, or its moldings, and rising to a finial or other ornament above.

Accommodation: The process by which the eye changes focus from one distance to another.

Accordion doors: A door constructed with joined portions of wood that will fold together.

Acetate: A fiber woven into carpeting, upholstery and drapes made from cellulose that has been chemically treated.

Achievement: In heraldry, a complete display of armorial bearings; as, the escutcheon with its accompanying crest, motto or mottos, and supporters, if any.

Acknowledgement: A formal notice of acceptance of an order that usually states delivery date.

Acorn: A design that resembles an acorn. In three-dimensional ornamentation used as a finial and pendant.

Acoustic: Used with a basic sound property.

Acoustical: Used in the control of sound.

Acoustical tile: Tiles or sheets that are acoustical absorbents.

Acoustics: The science of the control and transmission of sound. The unit of measure of sound is the decibel. Zero decibels is no sound. Normal conversation is 45 to 60 decibels. Hearing injury can occur at more than 100 decibels .

Acrolith: (A) A statue or figure in relief of which only the head, hands, and feet are of stone, the rest being of wood, or other material. (B) By extension, such a figure of which the extremities are of finer material than the rest, as of marble applied to inferior stone.

Acropodium: A pedestal for a statue, especially when large and high and adorned with unusual richness. A terminal pedestal or gain when resting upon representations of the human foot, or even of the feet of animals, is

sometimes specially called acropodium; but the term in this sense is inaccurate and has no classical warrant.

Acrotherium: (A) In classical architecture, properly, a pedestal for a statue or similar decorative feature at the apex, or at each of the lower corners of a pediment. None of ancient times remains in place; but in neoclassic work they are frequent. (B) By extension, from the preceding definition, but improperly, a statue or other decorative feature supported on such a pedestal.

Acrylic fibers: Man-made fibers with the soft, warm appearance of wool when used as a surface fiber in rugs and carpets.

Acrylics: Acrylic and modacrylic carpet fibers. Acrylic fiber contains at least 85% by weight of acrylonitrile units. Modacrylic fiber contains between 35%-85% by weight of acrylonitrile. Acrylic fibers are available only as staple. The spun yarns have the closest resemblance to wool of any synthetic. Acrylic fibers were introduced in carpets about 10 years after the advent of nylon. At first they were sometimes blended with modacrylic fibers as a guard against potential flammability. However, due to improvements in composition, the latest acrylic fibers are no more flammable than wool, and carpets with 100% acrylic pile are now quite common. Acrylics have the same soft, warm, luxurious appearance as wool and are used frequently as a substitute for wool. Their characteristics are good resilience, good resistance to abrasion, good texture retention, and good cleanability.

Adaptation: The process by which the visual system becomes accustomed to more or less light than it was exposed to during an immediately preceding period. It results in a change in the sensitivity of the eye to light.

Addorsed: Usually two animal figures placed symmetrically back to back. Commonly seen on capitals.

Adelphi: Trade name used by the Adam brothers.

Adhesive: A substance capable of bonding materials together by surface attachment. It is a general term and includes all cements and glues.

Adhesive, type I, fully waterproof: Forms a bond that will withstand full weather exposure and will be unaffected by microorganisms; bond shall be of such quality that specimens will withstand shear and cyclic boil tests specified in PS 51-71.

Adhesive, type II, water-resistant: Forms a bond that will retain practically all of its strength when occasionally subjected to a thorough wetting and drying; bond shall be of such quality that specimens will withstand the coad soak test specified in PS 51-71.

Adsorption: Physical or chemical attachment of thin layers of molecules onto the surface of liquids or solids with which they are in contact. An example is the initial adsorption of dyestuff molecules from the dissolved phase onto the fiber surface, which comprises the first step in the dyeing process.

Aedicule: Framing of a window or door with two columns or piers and supporting a lintel or pediment. In classical architecture, a shrine framed by two columns and supporting an entablature and pediment.

Aerugo: The composition formed upon ancient bronzes by exposure; usually being carbonate of copper, but differing in composition according to the nature of the metal or the soil in which it may have been buried.

Affinity: Attractive force between substances or particles causing them to combine chemically. An example is the affinity of acid dyes for nylon fiber.

Affronted: Usually two animal figures placed symmetrically facing each other. Commonly seen on capitals.

Agate ware: A blending of clays, resembling agate, through a process which has been adopted by Wedgewood.

Air Fitting: (Air bonnet, Air hood, Air saddle, Air box) A fitting which is mounted to an air handling luminaire and connects to the primary air duct by flexible ducting. It normally contains one or two volume controls.

A Giorno: Same as A jour; the Italian form of the phase.

Ajarcara: In Spanish architecture, ornamental relief in brickwork.

A jour: In French, pierced through, so that light shines through from side to side; said of carving when the background is pierced at intervals, or cut entirely away, so that the scroll or other ornament remains detached. In ornamental art the term is sometimes employed when the background is transparent, as when enamels or glass are fitted in to form it.

Ajoure: (French) A design consisting of pierced holes in ceramics metal, wood, or other material.

Alabaster: (A) A variety of gypsum; a sulfate of lime more or less translucent and of a prevailing white color, though often clouded and veined with brownish red and other tints. It is soft enough to be readily cut with a knife. A variety brought from Derbyshire in the south of England is used for altar rails in churches and similar decorative adjuncts to buildings, but its softness prevents its being durable. The Italian variety, which as exported, is more nearly white, is used chiefly for small vases, statuettes, and the like, which are called Florentine Marbles. (B) A variety of calcite known as the calcareous or Oriental alabaster, and supposed to be the Alabastrites of the ancient writers. This material, which is much harder than that in sense A, was very largely used in the works of the Romans of antiquity, and quarries in Egypt have been drawn upon in modern times for buildings in Cairo, and even in Europe. The quarries now known, however, would not furnish such large and perfect pieces of hard alabaster as have been found in the ruins of Rome, or as those which stand in the Church of S. Marco in Venice.

Alcove: (A) A recess opening out of a bedroom and intended to contain the bed; usually altogether, so that curtains at the opening of the alcove may conceal it entirely. This seems to be the primary use of the word, in English as in French. (B) A recess, niche, grotto, space enclosed by trees, or any such retired place.

Alder: A hard wood that is light-brown in color, finishes nicely and will not absorb water very well.

Alencon lace: A lace originating in France that is made of fine needlepoint.

Alkalinity test: A method of determining the feasibility of gluing down carpets on a concrete floor.

Alkyds: Plastics that are resistant to acids and oils and can withstand high temperatures. They are used for lacquer and enamel as a liquid and light switches, motor insulation,

and fuses as a solid. These plastics are very strong.

Allege: In French, a thinning or lightening of a part of a wall, as under a window, where the term covers the whole of the wall, usually much thinner, from the floor or the top of the opening below to the sill of the window above. There seems to be no English term for this; the inside of it forming the back or window back, and the exterior either remaining unmarked or constituting a sunken panel.

All-over design: A wallpaper or cloth designed with flowers or geometric shapes without a particular feature outlined.

Alternating Current: (AC) Flow of electricity which cycles or alternates direction many times per second. The number of cycles per second is referred to as frequency. Most common frequency used in this country is 60 Hertz (cycles per second).

Amaranth: A hard wood purplish-red in color used chiefly for marquetry and veneering.

Ambient lighting: General lighting, or lighting of the surround (as opposed to task lighting or the lighting of the object one is looking at). It can be produced by direct lighting from recessed surface or stem mounted luminaries, or by indirect lighting which is wall or stem mounted, built into furniture or free standing.

Amperes: (amps or A) The unit of measurement of electric current.

Amphora: A jar used by the Greeks and Romans with handles and a long neck.

Andirons: Metal frames or platforms used to hold firewood above the floor of a fireplace and thereby provide air circulation for combustion.

Angle of incidence: An angle perpendicular to the surface upon which a lighted ray falls.

Annealing: A strengthening process of flintglass by raising the temperature and then allowing it to cool off.

Antimacassar: A cloth doily or covering used as protection against dirt and dust on couches and chairs.

Antiques: Any item that was made prior to 1830 or before the machine age, also furniture and art objects that are 100 years or older are considered to be antiques. Antiques can be recognized by the deterioration of the surface, hand made nails or various markings. Often counterfeit antique furniture is produced so one must be careful when shopping.

Antiquing: An age stimulant used primarily on furniture, it is also known as distressing. Counterfeit antique dealers often use this method. The wood is severely damaged, acid-treated and beaten.

Antistatic: Ability of carpet to dissipate electrostatic charge thus reducing buildup of static electricity.

Applewood: A light colored wood more important for its fruit rather than for the small pieces of furniture it produces.

Appliance: Equipment such as, electrical fans and toasters that consume currents.

Applique: (French) An applied design, a sconce or wall bracket. An accessory decorative feature applied to an object or structure; the French term gradually becoming common in English. It may be as small as a bronze handle on the front of a drawer or shutter, or as large as a marble tabernacle set up against the wall of a room. In decorative art the term is applied to a piece of one substance set upon a surface of other material, for decorative effect.

Approved: Conforming to the requirements of the governing code enforcement agency.

Apron: A raised panel below a window sill. An addition or extension to the front of a stage platform.

Aquinch: An arch, a lintel, corbelling, or system of such members, built across the interior corner of two walls, as at the top of a tower, to serve as foundation for the diagonal or canted side of a superimposed octagonal spire or lantern. The squinch performs the functions of a pendentive.

Arch: (A) A structural member rounded vertically to span an opening or recess; in this sense the term is used either for a decorative or memorial building, of which an upward curving member forms the principal feature and spans a gate or passage below, or for the member itself, considered as a firm and resistant curved bar capable of bearing weight and pressure. In this, the original sense, a wicker device thrown across a street or passage and covered with foliage and flowers, is as much an arch as a more permanent structure. (B) A

mechanical means of spanning an opening by heavy wedge-shaped solids which mutually keep one another in place, and which transform the vertical pressure of the superincumbent load into two lateral components transmitted to the abutments.

ARCH: TRANSVERSE ARCH.

The shape is indifferent, although arches are generally curved. The width or thickness, horizontally, is also indifferent, although an arch which acts as a roof and covers much horizontal space is called a vault. The constructional arch has been known from great antiquity, but it was rarely used by the ancients except for drains or similar underground and hidden conveniences. It appears, however, that the Assyrian builders used it freely as a means of roofing their long and narrow palace walls. Assyrian vaults were built of unbaked brick put together with mortar, so that the anchor vault became a continuous and massive shell. On the other hand, the Etruscans from a very early time understood the principle of the arch so well that they built arches of cut stone in large separate voussoirs put together without mortar. For us, the Etruscans were the originators of the true self-supporting arch. It was adopted from them by the Romans; but both these nations confined themselves almost exclusively to the semicircular arch, both in spanning openings in walls and for purposes of vaulting. The pointed arch seems to have been known as early as the round arch. It is, indeed, an obvious way of making an arch which shall have greater height in proportion to its width, and which shall in this way be stronger, because having less outward thrust. Its use in pre-Gothic, as in early Islamic architecture, and in Romanesque buildings, as in S. Front at Perigueus, is merely occasional and because of some preference on the part of the individual builder. The three-centered arch and the four-centered arch are both much used in the transitional work of the sixteenth century in northern Europe. The segmental arch has hardly been used for decorative purposes, except occasionally in the Louis Quatorze style, before the present half century; it is now rather common in French work, and it may be that more could be made of it, architecturally speaking, than in the past. The flat arch is used commonly to produce a similitude of trabeated construction when in reality the stones accessible are too small for the great spans required. Thus, in Roman and neoclassic buildings, the epistyle or architrave between two columns is often made of separate voussoirs in this way, as in the Pantheon of Paris. Mechanically, an arch may be considered as any piece or assemblage of pieces so arranged over an opening that the vertical pressure of the supported load is transformed into two lateral inclined pressures on the abutments.

Considered in this light, then, the stone window head shown in Fig. 1 is truly an arch. The stone is wedge-shaped; and it will be readily seen that the load on it has a tendency to force this wedge down into the window opening by pushing the adjoining masonry away to the right and left, as shown by the arrows.

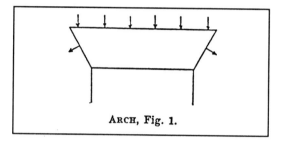

ARCH, Fig. 1.

An arch slightly more elaborate is the primitive arch shown in Fig. 2. Here two wedge-shaped stones lean against each other, and each one transmits pressures similar to those just described, the pressures at the respective upper ends counteracting each other. This form of arch may be compared to a pair of rafters whose tiebeam has been removed and its function fulfilled by a weight at the feet of the rafters. To go a step farther, we have an arch made of three stones, as shown in Fig. 3, each one of which is acting as an independent wedge tending to force its way inward, and so exerting a lateral pressure at each of its oblique ends, while the combination of all these six pressures results in a lateral push on each abutment as shown by the arrows. This lateral push, in Figs. 2 and 3, is similar to that in Fig. 1, from which it differs in direction,

owing to the inclination of the end pieces; were these more steeply inclined they would evidently exert a push more nearly vertical. Hence, the higher the arch in proportion to its span, the less lateral push will it exert. The foregoing considerations will be found to apply equally well to all of the arches shown in Fig. 2, or to any other similar construction of wedge-shaped pieces. It will also be observed that, in the case of two or more such wedges, each one is being acted upon by the adjoining pieces, which tend to force it outward; this tendency is overcome only by proper and more or less uniform distribution of the loads to be carried. The lateral pressure on the abutment is known as the trust, and resistance to this force was the subject of constant experiment in the church building of the Middle Ages, resulting in the elaborate systems of engaged and flying buttresses.

THREE POINTED ARCHES

Arch, Fig. 2.

Arches may be divided according to their form into the following classes:--

(a) The Flat Arch;

(b) The arch with one center; (1) semicircular or Round Arch; (2) Segmental Arch; (3) Horseshoe Arch.

(c) With two centers; (1) Equilateral Pointed Arch; (2) Lancet Arch; (3) Drop Arch or Blunt Pointed Arch; (4) Pointed Horseshoe Arch; (5)

Drop Arch in the second sense. These five varieties are what is known as pointed arches; the first three being those in use in many styles.

(d) With three centers; (1) Basket Handle Arch; (2) the round arch with reversed curve at crown. (e) With four centers; (1) that form of pointed arch in which two of the centers are on the springing line and two below; (2) that in which a two-centered arch is prolonged at top with a reversed curve. It is evident that a six-centered arch might be composed by giving to the form

(e) (1) a reversed curve as in the other instances; but such subdivisions may be continued indefinitely; thus a five-centered arch might be developed out of the basket handle arch; and so on.

An arch is divisible into the Haunches, or Reins, and the Crown. An arch is made up of Voussoirs, of which there may be one in the middle occupying the center of the crown and called a Keystone. The inner side of the arch ring is called the intrados. The outer side of the arch ring is called the Extrados, or back. When an arch is laid down on paper the horizontal line which passes through the center in the plane of the arch, if there is but one, or which connects two centers, and which (except in the segmental arches, one- or two-centered) marks the place at which the curve of the arch joins the vertical line of the abutment, is called the Springing Line. The height from the springing line to the intrados (or to the line which in a drawing represents the intrados) is the height or Rise; sometimes called the versed line. The width between the two points of juncture above mentioned is the Span. That part of an arch which forms a part of the face of the wall is called the face of the arch, or very commonly, the Archivolt. Parts of the construction immediately dependent upon or connected with an arch are the Abutment; Impost; Skew Back; Spandrel; Springer.

Archaic: Pertaining to or having the character of extremely early and primitive work. As applied to different branches of art, the term refers to different but specific periods; as, for example, in Greek art, to the formative period between the Heroic or Homeric Age, and the middle or end of the sixth century B.C. Archaic is distinguished from primitive art by its evidence of those definite progressive tendencies which give form to the later and more perfect art.

Architect: A person who designs, draws plans, and manages the construction of a building.

Architectural: (A) Pertaining to architecture; as, an architectural publication or drawing. (B) Having the character of a work of architecture; as, an architectural composition. (C) Composed or treated in accordance with the principles of architecture; as, an architectural decoration.

Architectural terra cotta: Clay that is burned and used in building units.

Architrave: A molded frame surrounding a window or door. The lowest part of an entablature.

Archivolt: A continuous architrave molding on the face of an arch.

Arc tube: An enclosure usually found on fluorescent, mercury, quartz or high-pressured sodium lamps, made of glass or ceramic.

Area rug: A rug smaller than a room-sized carpet.

Area: The length multiplied by the width determines the area.

Arita porcelain: Sixteenth century porcelain made in Arita, Japan with beautifully colored designs and overglazes. It was first exported in Europe in the seventeenth century and is also known as Imari ware.

Arkwright: One who makes arks and chests or signifies simply constructed, late medieval furniture.

Armoire: (French) Clothes wardrobe. A tall cabinet with two doors used to store clothes but was originally used to hide weapons.

Armorial china: Pieces of service porcelain with coats-of-arms and crests for decoration.

Arris: The sharp edge that results from two surfaces meeting.

Asbestos: A mineral of so fibrous a nature that it can be woven into a textile fabric, which is naturally incombustible; having also the quality of slow conduction of heat. Its chief use in building has been for the covering of steam pipes, etc.; and covering for floors has been made from the fiber. Asbestos has been declared a health hazard and is now banned from use in most building material.

Ash: A hard, flexible wood straw-colored and similar to oak in grain.

Ashlar: Masonry blocks hewn with even faces and square edges and laid in horizontal courses with vertical joints. This is in contrast to rubble or unhewn stone. (A) Squared and finished building stone; in recent times, especially, such stone when used for the face of a wall whose substance is made of inferior material. The term has usually a general signification, and a single piece would be called a block of ashlar; rarely, an ashlar. An attempt has been made to limit the term to stone which is set on its edge, that is to say, not on the quarry bed, and in this way to serve as a translation of the French adjectival phrase en delit; but there seems to be no authority for this limitation. (B) Attributively, and in combination, having the appearance of, or to be used in the place of, ashlar, as a veneer. (C) A vertical stud between the sloping roof and flooring in a garret or roof story, by a series of which vertical walls are provided for the sides of rooms, and the angular space near the eaves partitioned off either as waste space or as low closets. Such studding is more commonly spoken of collectively as ashlaring.

Assemblage: Art work that is assembled with driftwood, paper, and metal objects. The items used are usually things not considered as art materials.

Assembly: Combined functional parts that make cabinets and doors etc.

Astragal: Small circular section molding usually with bead and reel decoration.

Atelier: A workshop or studio; the French term naturalized in English for an artist's studio, and, especially, for one of those studios in which pupils are trained in any fine art.

Atlantes: Columns or supports carved in the form of male figures. Used extensively by German Baroque architects.

Attached cushion: Cushion permanently bonded to the back of carpets and rugs by the manufacturer.

Attic story: A room or upper story in a building or house often directly under the roof. In classical architecture, a story above the main entablature of a building.

Attribute: An object, as a weapon, a flower, or the like, considered as expressing the character or authority of a divinity; thus the dove is a recognized attribute of Venus in Roman and modern mythology.

Aubusson: A carpet or tapestry, handwoven, without a pile. Named after the French city famous for this weave since the fifteenth century.

Austrial shades: Curtains that can be raised and lowered with cords. They are sheer and have horizontal swags for effect.

Average stiffness: Force required to stretch fibers 1% in length, expressed in grams per denier. Related to Young's Modulus.

Avodire: An African wood, light yellow in color with a clear grain. It is used primarily as a guise for furniture making.

Axial plan: A building planned along an axis or longitudinally.

Axis: (A) In architectural drawing, a central line, not necessarily intended to form a part of the finished drawing, but laid down as a guiding line from which may be measured figure dimensions of rooms, the widths of openings, etc. A primary axis may pass through the middle of the Ground Plan. There may be as many subsidiary axes as the different rooms, wings, pavilions, or other primary parts of the building may require. (B) An imaginary line to which is referred the parts of an existing building or the relations of a number of buildings to one another. Thus, in Greek architecture, the buildings standing on the Acropolis of Athens, or those within the sacred enclosure at Epidauros or Olympia, have each a distinctly marked axis, but have no common axis that modern explorers have been able to fix. Such buildings are, indeed, set at angles with one another so obvious that the idea of a common axis is precluded. On the other hand, the great temple at Karnak in Egypt has a bent or deviated axis; that is to say, while the first three or four halls and courts have evidently been carefully arranged upon one axis, those that follow are arranged upon another axis, making a very slight angle with the former one. A similar deflection occurs in many medieval churches, and a legend exists, very hard to verify, according to which this change of direction from the nave to the choir is intended to suggest the reclining of the Saviour's head upon the cross. All careful planning is done with some reference to an axis, but the designers of different schools disagree widely as to the value to be given to the placing of buildings and parts of buildings accurately upon an axis, or as it is called, following the French term, En Axe. (C) One of three perpendicular lines intersecting at a common point in space.

Axminster carpet: One of the basic weaves that originated in the 1700s in the town of Axminster, England. Unlike the Wilton weave, almost all the pile yarns appear on the surface of Axminster carpeting. The pile tufts are anchored by stiff weft shots of jute, kraftcord, or synthetic fibers running across the width of the carpet. The surface yarns are usually cut and of one height. They are woven in geometric and floral patterns in combinations of colors and patterns.

Axonometric projection: A drawing showing an object or building in three dimensions. The plan is organized at an appropriate angle and all dimensions on both the horizontal and vertical plane are to scale. Diagonals and curves on the vertical plane are distorted.

Azulejos: Glazed pottery tiles used in Spanish and Latin American buildings. They are usually painted with bright colors and florals and exaggerated decorative patterns.

B

"B" size sheet: 11" x 17".

Baccarat: Crystal glassware first made in 1818 in France. It is exceptionally beautiful and much sought after.

Bachelors chest: An eighteenth century English chest with a leaf under the top that opens to provide a desktop.

Back: To provide with a proper back; to finish the back of; especially, to trim or adjust the back or top of a rafter, joist, or the like, to the proper level of the whole tier. Often with a preposition, back priming: a coat of paint applied to the backside and edges of woodwork or exterior siding to prevent excessive absorption of moisture.

Backgammon table: A game table that was 44 inches square and had drawers on both ends. It dates as far back as the Middle Ages and was very popular in the eighteenth century.

Backing: Materials (fabrics or yarns) comprising the back of the carpet as opposed to the carpet pile or face. (a) Primary back: in tufting, a woven or nonwoven fabric in which the pile yarn is inserted by the tufting needles. Usually woven or nonwoven polypropylene woven jute for carpet and often cotton duck for scatter rugs. (b) Secondary back: fabric laminated to the back of carpet to reinforce and increase dimensional stability. Usually woven jute or woven or nonwoven polypropylene. Backings of woven carpets are the "construction yarns" comprising chain warp, stuffer warp, and shot or fill which are interwoven with the face yarn during carpet fabric formation. The material that forms the back of the carpet. It can be of wool, kraftcord, jute, cotton, rayon, polypropylene, or other material or a combination of materials depending on the dye and the quality of the carpet.

Backing out: Wide, shallow groove machined in back surface of members.

Back order: An order that is to be shipped sometime in the future.

Back painting: A procedure in which a glass pane is made transparent by gluing on print and painting or tinting the back.

Back priming: A coat of paint applied to the backside and edges of woodwork or exterior siding to prevent excessive absorption of moisture.

Back putty: After the glass has been face puttied, it is turned over and putty is run into any voids that may exist between the glass and the wood parts.

Back seams: Installation seams made with the carpet turned over or face down. Opposite of face seams made with the carpet face up. Both of course are on the back of the carpet.

Baffle: An opaque or translucent element that serves to shield a light source from direct view at certain angles, or serves to absorb unwanted light.

Baguette: A frame made with a bead molding. A small semicircular section molding.

Baker's rack: A stand used to exhibit art objects but was originally used to display bread. It was developed in France, has four shelves and is made of wrought iron.

Balance: Equal value of weight on the right and left sides of a room.

Balancing species: A species, of similar density, to achieve balance

by equalizing the rate of moisture absorption or emission.

Balcony: A platform projecting from wall, door or a window sill and enclosed with a railing. It may be cantilevered or supported by brackets or columns.

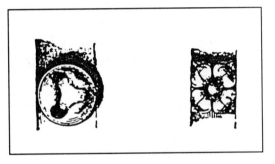

Ballast: An auxiliary device consisting of induction windings wound around a metal core and sometimes includes a capacitor for power correction. It is used with fluorescent and HID lamps to provide the necessary starting voltage and to limit the current during operation.

Ball flower: A globular ornament frequently occurring in the hollow moldings of English Gothic architecture. It suggests a flower with three, or rarely four, petals nearly closed over an inner ball, and is repeated at short intervals to give points of light in the darkness of the hollow. Isolated four-part flowers are sometimes found in late Norman work.

Balloon framing: In the United States, a system of framing wooden buildings in which the corner posts and studs are continuous in one piece from sill to roof plate, the intermediate joists being carried by girts spiked to, or let into, the studs, the pieces being secured only by nailing, without the use of mortices and tenons, or the like.

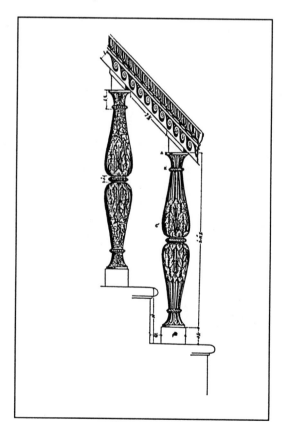

Baluster: (Banister) One of a set of small pillars that supports a handrail (or balustrade) on a stairway. It is also used as decoration on furniture.

Balustrade: A short series of pillars or balusters terminated on top with a rail.

Bamboo furniture, imitation: Furniture turned out of beech and simulated to look like bamboo. It has been popular since the eighteenth century.

Banding: A piece of wood used for decoration on furniture of a different color or grain.

Banister-back chair: An open back chair with splats or banisters.

Banjo clock: An American pendulum clock from the nineteenth century in the shape of a banjo.

Banquette: (French) Bench. A bench or a built-in seat with upholstery.

Bar: An area, usually in the den or the family room, used to store liquor or other beverages. The bar's table surface can be used to serve condiments and cabinets would be helpful to keep things organized.

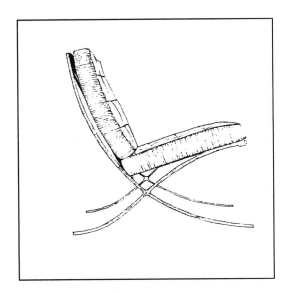

Barcelona chair: Classic chair made of chromium steel, popular with architects and upholstered with leather cushions. It was designed in 1929 by Mies van der Rohe. It is still popular.

Barometer: An instrument, popular in the eighteenth century, used to measure the pressure of the atmosphere.

Barrel chair: A deep concave backed chair that is upholstered.

Barrier-free design: A design for handicapped people used to make movement easier. An example of this kind of design would be a ramp in addition to stairs. These designs were implemented in 1971 due to the American National Standards Institution.

Barriers: Obstructions which interfere with the intended use of a space.

Bars, to fill a given opening: It may be either open or glazed.

Basaltes: Earthenware made by Josiah Wedgewood and copied by Spode.

Base block: A block of any material, generally with little or no ornament, forming the lowest member of a base, or itself fulfilling the functions of a base; specifically, a member sometimes applied to the foot of a door or window trim.

Base line: (A) In architectural drawings, the lowest horizontal line; the line which marks the base or bottom of the design; especially, in perspective, the trace of the picture plane on the ground plane. (B) In engineering and surveying, the first line determined upon, located, and measured as a base from which other lines, angles and distances are laid out or computed in surveying or plotting a piece of ground for a map or plan.

Base-shoe: Molding applied to a wall where it meets the floor in order to prevent damage.

Baseboard: A board skirting the lower edge of a wall.

Basement: (A) The lower part of the wall or walls of any building, especially when divided from the upper portions in an architectural way, as by a different material, a different and perhaps more solid architectural treatment, smaller and fewer windows, or the like. The basement may occupy only a small part of the whole height of the structure, or it may be even more than half of that height, as in some palaces of the Italian Renaissance, especially in northern Italy. It frequently happens that there is a double basement; that is to say, the basement proper, serving as a foil and a support to the more elaborate story or stories above, has itself a still more massive basement, probably without openings. (B) The story which comes, in the construction of the building, behind the piece of wall above described; in this sense, an abbreviation of the term "basement story." Originally,

this story would have its floor almost exactly on a level with the street without, or with the courtyard; but in some buildings it is raised several steps above the street, and in others its floor is some distance below the street, as, notable, in city dwelling houses.

Bas-Relief: (A) A form of sculpture in which the figures project but slightly from the general background; low relief; as, for example, in the frieze of the Parthenon. (B) Any sculptured work thus executed in low relief. Bas-relief is especially used as an adjunct to architecture. The contrasting treatment of sculpture is high relief or *alto-rilievo*.

Bathroom: A room equipped with a toilet, shower and/or bathtub and a sink.

Batik: A fabric whose pattern is made by a resist wax printing process. A method of partially dyeing fabrics, covering a part of it with wax to repel the dye. The wax then is melted in boiling water

Batiste: A lightweight, frequently printed, sheer fabric.

Battersea enamel: A method of fusing into a metal base a painted or printed enameled design.

Batting: Stuffing for quilts or comforters made of cotton or wool.

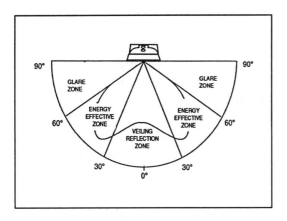

Batwing distribution: Candlepower distribution which serves to reduce glare and ceiling reflections by having its maximum output in the 30° to the 60° zone from the vertical and with a candlepower at nadir (0°) being 65% or less than maximum candlepower. The shape is similar to a bat's wing. In fluorescent luminaries the batwing distribution is generally found only in the plane perpendicular to the lamps.

Baxter prints: A patented method of oil-color printing discovered by George Baxter in 1835. A block for each color is added.

Bay window: Originally, a large window, often of many parts, or subdivisions, and related to the modern Italian term, _balcone._ The word "bay" in its two senses, first, of a recess or opening, and second, of one of many subdivisions of a long building, seems to have suggested the use of the same term, bay, for an enclosed structure which would form a recess, or opening, and which, by means of its projection from the exterior wall, would seem to constitute one subdivision, or "bay," as seen from the exterior. This structure was then called bay window, and the term has no closer or more exact signification than is here explained. In modern times an attempt has been made to distinguish the bay window as a structure resting on the ground from the oriel window as a structure corbelled out from the wall of the building. Also a distinction has been attempted between bow window with a curved outline in its plan, and bay window with a broken or polygonal outline. As generally understood, in modern country houses and the like, the bay window is of the nature of an enclosed loggia by means of which a view can be had along the face of the walls on each side, and the sun can perhaps be let into a room which would otherwise not receive it; it may be two or three feet deep, or it may be as large as a moderate-sized room with a projection from the wall even greater than its measurement along the face of the wall. In some cases, the bay window is separated from the room which it adjoins by a decided break in the ceiling, as by an arch or transom, and the ceiling of the bay window may be lower than that of the room. In other cases the ceiling is continuous, and the bay window is really a prolongation, or widening, of the room.

BCF: Bulked continuous filament. Continuous strands of synthetic fiber formed into yarn bundles of a given number of filaments and texturized to increase bulk and cover. Texturizing changes the straight filaments into kinked or curled configurations.

Beading: Long fiber fuzz on fabrics. Caused by fiber snagging and inadequate anchorage.

Bead molding: Cylindrical molding with ornament resembling a string of beads. Common in Romanesque architecture.

Beakhead: Roll molding ornamented with a row of bird or animal heads. Common in Norman architecture.

Beam: A transverse horizontal timber used in roof construction. Horizontal timbers supporting floor or ceiling joists. A piece or member of which the transverse dimensions are small relative to its length; intended generally to be supported at two or more points to resist forces acting in a direction normal to its axis; but sometimes secured at one end only and sometimes acting as a member of a truss, in which case its purpose may be that of a strut, but always occupying a more or less horizontal position. By extension, however, the term is still used to designate any piece of a form intended primarily for the purpose described although put to another use: thus, a steel column may be constructed of channel beams, which would then be set on end. Beams of wood or stone are usually rectangular in cross section, or nearly so. Those of iron or steel have different cross sections, but are generally composed of a top and a bottom flange connected by a thin vertical web. The most common forms are the I beam, the channel beam, the Z beam, and the deck or bulb beam. Iron and steel beams are now rolled in one piece up to a depth of 2 feet. The larger sizes are made up of several pieces, and known as built beams and box beams. A large beam is frequently known as a Girder, irrespective of its use.

Beam: Large, horizontal cylinders or spools. Warp yarns are wound on beams and located on line in back of the weaving operation.

Beam: Light rays that are almost parallel.

Bearing: (A) That part of a lintel, beam, or similar horizontal weight-carrying member which rests upon a column, pier, or wall. Thus, it may be required that a beam of a certain size, and with a certain span, should have at each end an 8-inch bearing. (B) The whole length or span of a lintel, girder, or similar structure between the two points of support, that is the whole distance between the two bearings, in sense A. Of

these two meanings, the second is the one most often seen in untechnical writing, but in specifications and the like the word is more commonly limited to the meaning A, and the word Span is used for the distance between the two points.

Beauvais: A French city that is popular for its tapestries, manufactured there since 1644. The tapastry was first sponsored by Louis XIV.

Bedding in putty: Glazing whereby a thin layer of putty or bedding compound is placed in the glass rabbet, the glass inserted and pressed onto the bed.

Bed molding: Molding that occurs between the corona and the frieze of an entablature.

Bedroom, master: The largest bedroom in a house or apartment.

Bed-sitting room: A combination bedroom and sitting room. It is a bedroom with a small living room area.

Bedspread: A decorative covering for a bed.

Beech: A hard wood, whitish to red-brown in color, which has a fine grain and is extemely dense. Beech is mainly used for flooring.

Belleek: A lustrous porcelain named after the Irish city where it is made.

Bench mark: A fixed reference mark from which heights and levels are reconned in surveying or in laying out grounds and buildings. It is usually indicated by a notch or mark on a stone or stake firmly set at a given point of the plan.

Bennington: A factory which produces gray salt-glazed stoneware pottery. The pottery is often decorated with blue floral designs and was copied from English ware. Pottery is more dense than porcelain.

Bent needles: (A) Needles in the tufting machine permanently pushed out of place causing a streak or grinning, running lengthwise because of off-standard tuft spacing across the width. (B) A needle in the Jacquard that is out of alignment with punched holes in pattern cards.

Bentwood furniture: A process of bending wet wood discovered by Michael Thonet. Elm is often used because of its malleablity.

Bergere: An armchair made in the Louis XV style with upholstered

sides, rounded back and a carved frame. This style is from the eighteenth century and is still popular.

Betty lamp: An eighteenth century oil lamp which can either hang from the ceiling or stand on the floor.

Bevel: (A) The inclination of one face to another; the divergence of one part or face from the plane of another, or from a perpendicular to that plane. Thus, if a strut is to be inclined to the plate on which it is to stand, its lower end must be bevelled in order to have an even, uniform bearing; door saddles usually have their edges bevelled; parts of masonry may be bevelled so as to form a splay about a window opening. (B) A face making a bevel in sense A. (C) An instrument consisting of two flat straight-edged legs (one or both being usually slotted) and a clamping screw by which they are set at any desired angle. Used chiefly to lay off or measure a bevel, as defined above.

Bias: A cut on fabric across the warp edge to the selvage in a 45° degree angle.

Bibelot: (French) A small art object for decoration or personal use. According to comedian George

Carlin this would fall under the general catagory, "stuff."

Bibliotheque: A bookcase cabinet with doors. French for library.

Bidet: A fixture in the bathroom that provides quick bathing of perineal areas after using the toilet.

Billet: Molding made up of several bands of raised cylinders or square pieces at regular intervals. Common in Romanesque architecture.

Bill of lading: A receipt for shipped goods to a certain destination.

Bill of materials: A list of parts represented in a drawing. In CAD this ability is usually automated.

Binder: Material, or a member, used to bind; specifically: (A) A binding beam or binding joist; a girder to support floor joists. (B) Loose material used to bind together other pieces or materials; thus, sand or earth may be used as a binder for the crushed stone in road building. (C) In masonry, a header; a bond stone. (D) An oil or resin which serves to form a film.

Binder bar: A commercially available strip of metal or vinyl installed over a carpet edge for protection against unraveling and wear.

Binding: A commercially available cloth tape that is sewn over a carpet edge as a protection against unraveling and wear.

Birch: A hard wood used largely for expensive furniture. Although it doesn't have much color it has an extremely nice finish and can imitate walnut or mahogany.

Birdcage: A term used to describe the formation of either wooden or metal posts set into a tread in a spiral configuration as a newel post supporting a stair hand rail.

Birdcage support: A cage-like device that connects the top of a table to the base. The top then can be slanted when it is not in use.

Birdseye: A small central spot with wood fibers arranged around it so as to give the appearance of an eye.

Bird's-eye maple: A maple wood light brownish-yellow in color. It is decorated with dark brown circles.

Bisque: Fired but unglazed ceramics. It is also known as biscuit.

Blackamoor: A table base made from a candlestand or a figure of a dark-skinned person.

Blanc de Chine: Ming Dynasty porcelain made from white or translucent ivory.

Bleeding: Removal of color from carpet or other fabrics by a liquid, usually water, and subsequent staining of areas adjacent to the wet area, or of other materials in contact with the wet area.

Blind: Having no windows; said of a building or part of a building which usually has them. Thus, a blind clerestory or a blind nave is one where the aisles rise so high on either side as to prevent the opening of windows above the aisle roofs.

Blind, rolling: (A) Any blind of partially flexible structure, as of small strips of bamboo or the like, arranged to roll up, usually at the top of a window. (B) Sometimes, by extension from rolling slat or slats, one in which the slats are not fixed but free to rotate each on its own axis, the whole set being held together by a strip secured to each by a loop of wire.

Blind stitching: Invisible stiching sewn onto fabric.

Blind, venetian: A blind of which the slats are made to open and close; especially, a hanging blind, of which the slats are held together by strips of webbing and controlled by cords so that they may be opened or closed at will, and so that they may be drawn together and packed closely above the window.

Blind window: A nonfunctional window applied to a wall for decorative purpose or fenestration.

Blister: A defect in the form of a slight projection of a surface detached from the body of the material, caused in manufacturing or by weather or other agencies, as the protuberance sometimes formed on the face of a casting, due to the presence of an air bubble just below the surface; or the loose, slightly raised portions of a coat of paint which have become detached from the material to which the paint has been applied, due to defective workmanship or other causes.

Block, concrete: Concrete blocks used in the construction of buildings that are hollow or solid.

Blockfront: A chest of Chippendale style furniture made from mahogany. The front had three vertical panels with the sides convex and the middle concave.

Block printing: A block of wood with engraving of picture of patterns. Also can be done with fabrics or wallpaper.

Blow molding: Thermoplastic materials formed by stretching and hardening plastic to a mold. Molten thermoplastic is shaped and put into a mold, air blown, cooled, and removed from the mold.

Blueprinting: A process of inexpensively reproducing an original drawing. This process allows the designer, who draws plans, details and other types of drawings on transparent or translucent paper, to have one or 100 copies to give to the client and contractors, and still protect the valuable original.

Board: (A) A piece of lumber before gluing for width or thickness. (B) A slab of wood cut to a more or less uniform shape, and thin as compared to its width and length. Specifically, such a piece of lumber not more than about 1 1/4 inches thick.

Board measure: The standard system for the measurement of lumber. A board foot is a square foot one inch thick, and hence the equivalent of 144 cubic inches. A 3" x 4" stud measures one board foot

per foot of length; a 6" x 12" beam measures 6 board feet per foot of length. No allowance is made for loss by sawing, planing, or other dressing; 7/8"planed boards are reckoned as 1" thick. Lumber is sold by the M or thousand board feet. The board foot, the "hundred," and the M or thousand are the only units in common use.

Bobbin: A spool-like device made of various materials, shapes, and constructions with a head at one or both ends and a hole through its length or barrel for placement on a spindle or skewer. It is used to hold yarn for spinning, weaving, or sewing.

Bobbinet: A net that is hexagonal and made with a lace machine.

Bobeche: (French) Candle socket. A glass ring that is placed over a candleholder to catch the melting wax.

Body: (A) The larger, or more central mass of a building having varied parts, as a church. (B) The shaft, or plain upright part, of a pillar or pier of any sort. (C) Solidity, mass, thickness, and the like, taken in the abstract; thus, it may be said that a paint lacks body. (D) The solid, firm or full feel of a fabric.

Body color: A color or paint having body, i.e., rendered heavy and opaque; especially, in water color work, a paint mixed with white.

Bohemian glass: Eighteenth century glass that resembles rock crystal. It is finely etched and was first displayed in Bohemia.

Boiserie: (French) Carved woodwork. French word for a decorated and carved paneling and woodwork. Commonly used in seventeeth and eighteenth century French architecture and decorated with bas-relief carving.

Bokhara rug: A Turkish rug made with fine hair. The pattern is usually one of octagons on a brownish-red or tan backround.

Bolection molding: Molding used to hide the joint between two surfaces with different levels.

Bolster: A bed or couch pillow that is long and cylindrical.

Bolster work: A form of rusticated masonry in which the rounded projecting blocks or rustications bear a fancied resemblance to bolsters.

Bolt: A pin or rod used either to secure two or more parts or members permanently together; or movable, as for a temporary fastening; or fixed, to afford a more or less temporary support or means of attachment. More specifically: (A) A pin or bar, generally of wrought iron or steel, to secure parts or members together, having a head worked on one end and a screw thread and nut at the other, or sometimes nuts at both ends. Distinguished from a rod as connecting two or more members in immediate contact, and, therefore, as being shorter. (B) A pin, hook, or large screw driven or let into a wall, or the like, as a means-generally temporary-of support or suspension. Hardly to be distinguished from a spike or screw in the ordinary sense, except as being larger or of more elaborate form.

Boltel: In medievil architecture a convex rounded molding. By extension from the above meaning, the coping of a gable, generally forming a quadrant.

Bombe: A front, usually found on cabinets, that are curved in shape. This was popular during the eighteenth century and is still popular.

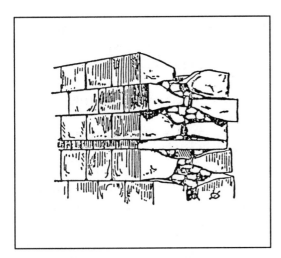

Bond: Any substance or object that attaches or adheres between two things.

Bond: The connection of two or more parts or members which overlap and are made to adhere more or less closely; a piece or pieces used for that purpose. Specifically: (A) In carpentry, (1) the securing or framing of two or more timbers together by means of a third crossing them; (2) the timbers, considered collectively, placed in or on the walls, and which act to stiffen and bind the parts of a building, as wall plates, templets. (B) In masonry, (1) the tie or binding of the various parts or pieces made by laying one piece across two or more pieces or parts; (2) a piece of material used for that purpose; hence, (3) the entire system of bonding or breaking joints as used in a masonry structure, for example, a wall may be said to be built in English bond. Incorrectly, the securing or holding together of the parts of a masonry structure by the mortar or similar adhesive material. (C) In roofing, (1) the amount by which one slate, tile, or shingle overlaps the second course below. (2) Sometimes the distance from the nail of one to the lower edge of the course above. In bonding masonry, the following names are given to the various pieces of stone or brick: Binder; Header, one laid lengthwise across a wall, generally perpendicular with the face. Perpend, in stonework, a binder extending entirely through, from face to face (French parpaing). Stretcher, one laid lengthwise parallel with the face. Through, same as perpend.

Bonded urethane cushion: A carpet cushion made from urethane trim, generated from urethane foam product manufacture, which has been granulated and bonded to form a porous foam material and fabricated into foam sheets.

Bone china: China that is naturally white in color, made from clay and bone ash.

Bonheur-du-jour: (French) Small desk with a cabinet on top.

Bonnet top: A broken section of furniture that covers the top from the front to the back.

Borax firm: A firm which produces cheap, poorly designed and inexpensive furniture.

Boston rocker: A rocking chair of dense wood similiar to a Windsor chair. It is decorated with tiny spindles and curves up in the back and down in the front.

Boucle: A loose thread of yarn having a curly, buckled appearance when used to make cloth.

Bouillotte: (French) A small gallery edged table. A foot-warmer.

Boulle marquetry: Ornate inlays of marble, pewter, brass or mother-of-pearl, originated in France.

Bow: A deviation flatwise from a straight line drawn from end to end of a piece. It is measured at the point of greatest distance from the straight line.

Bow compass: A device for drawing circles and arcs. This can substitute for a circle template, and will work with both pencil and ink.

Bowfront: An eighteenth century curved design on chests and toilettes also called a swell front.

Bowtell: A convex molding.

Box beam: A square or rectangular beam that is hollow.

Boxing: The joining piece of fabric between the top and the bottom of a cushion.

Brace: A piece or member, generally long as compared to its lateral dimensions, used to stiffen or steady another member or structure; specifically;

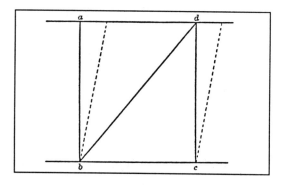

A bar introduced into a framework to prevent distortion or change of shape, usually a diagonal in a quadrilateral. It may act either by tension or by compression. The quadrilateral *abcd* may change its shape by the rotation of its sides about the joints. If the rigid diagonal brace *bd* is introduced and firmly attached, deformation is rendered impossible except by rupture of the parts. If the rectangle is exposed to deforming forces in two directions, i.e., to the right or to the left in the diagram; a single rigid brace firmly attached to the frame will prevent change of shape, but it is customary in such case to introduce two diagonals, both ties or both struts or compression members, as the case may be, which facilitate construction. If the four sides of the quadrilateral are rigid members, the diagonals will be ties. If two of the opposite sides are tension members, the braces will be struts.

Bracing: The operation of strengthening a framed or other structure by means of braces; or any system or aggregation of braces. The general principle upon which bracing depends for its efficiency is that of the triangle, whose shape cannot be changed without breaking, bending, or altering the length of one or more of its sides.

Bracket: A member prepared for carrying a weight which overhangs or projects, as a projecting story of a building, or a shelf. This is the general term; and although it would not be applied, often, to a cantilever, a corbel, a *cul-de-lampe*, or a modillion except carelessly, it covers all varieties which have no specific names of their own. The action of the bracket is twofold: it pulls outward along the line of the horizontal top bar or edge, and presses inward more solidly at the foot. If, therefore, a bracket is secured to a wall along the whole height of its vertical member, the more the horizontal member above is loaded, as with a balcony, bay window, or the like, the more of a pull is exercised upon the wall immediately below this projecting member. This may even become dangerous; and it is, therefore, customary to make the bracket a part of a floor or other horizontal member which can resist a strong outward tendency. The term is applied also to small movable objects which project from walls so as to resemble distantly the architectural bracket. Thus, a gas fixture for a wall opening, and, equally, a support for a bust, or vase, hung upon a hook, received the name.

Bracket clock: A clock which sits on top of a wall bracket.

Braided rug: A woven rug made from strands of fabric in different colors. Reversible oval or round rugs produced from braided strips of new or used material.

Brake: A machine that allows wide sheets or plates to be bent.

Branch circuit: An electrical circuit running from a service panel having its own overload protection device.

Branch: (A) A member or part of a system or structure which diverges from the main portion; especially in heating, ventilation, plumbing, and the like; a smaller or subordinate duct or pipe extending from the main line for whatever purpose. (B) A piece of piping having two or more arms by which a branch is connected with another or with the main line.

Brass: A metal alloy consisting of copper and zinc.

Brasses: Furniture accessories such as pulls and handles, considered a slang term.

Brass furniture: Furniture, usually beds, with brass ornamentation.

Breakfront: A cabinet with drawers on the bottom and glass doors on the top. The middle portion is a few inches extended from the sides.

Breaking strength: Maximum stretching force that can be applied to fabric, yarn, carpet or other material before it breaks. Sometimes expressed as pounds force to break a standard sized test specimen in the ASTM Grab Test.

Brewster chair: A seventeenth century armchair with a rush or plank seat, posts, and spindles. The chair is American Jacobean style and was named for William Brewster who was a Plymouth colonist.

Bric-a-brac: Any object that is artistic or rare and is used for decoration. A dust collector. See *bibelot*.

Brick: (A) A regularly shaped piece of clay hardened in the sun or by the heat of a kiln and intended for building; commonly one of very many pieces of uniform size. The term is usually limited to pieces of clay not very thin and flat, which latter are called tiles; the ordinary brick is, as in parts of the United States, about 2 1/2"by 4" x 8", or, as in parts of Europe, about 2 5/8" by 4 3/8" by 9." Bricks made for facework, that is, the smoother and more elegant facing of the exterior of a wall, are made of many shapes and colors and commonly laid with mortar joints much smaller than those between the common bricks in the same wall. Molded bricks are made in a great number of patterns, and so arranged as to form, when laid up in the wall, continuous lines of molding, curves of an arch, and the like, or patterns in relief, and even to the extent of having a raised leafage or the like upon their faces. (B) The material, baked clay, in small pieces in a general sense.

Brick: Plastic that is burned into clay, shaped into a rectangular prism, and fired in a kiln.

Bricklaying: The art and practice of laying bricks in masonry. As the purpose of bricklaying, when simple and confined to ordinary walls, is merely to produce a solid, almost homogeneous mass of small pieces of baked clay held together by strong mortar, the chief training given to a bricklayer is to lay bricks rapidly with fair accuracy and tolerable neatness. Face bricks are laid by workers especially trained for that purpose, or who have become especially skilful. The more difficult parts of bricklaying are the laying up of flues, where no lining, as of earthenware pipe, is to be used; the building of the throats of chimneys, upon the accurate adjustment of which much depends; and the doing of corbelled-out work with chimney tops and the like, all of which may be considered, together with the laying of molded brick, as unusual and ornamental parts of the trade.

Bridging: (A) A piece, or pieces, of scantling, or heavier timber, placed transversely between other timbers to stiffen them and to distribute the weight of a load more evenly on them. (B) The setting of bridging pieces, or of any pieces which are to serve as struts or stiffeners between parallel beams. When the bridging between the floor joists forms a series of X's, it is often called Cross Bracing and Cross Bridging, in the United States.

Brightness (Luminance): The degree of apparent lightness of a surface; its brilliancy; concentration of candlepower. Brightness is produced by either a self-luminous object, by light energy transmitted through objects or by reflection. Unit of measurement of brightness is the footlambert (fl).

Bringing forward: The operation of so priming or painting old work and new, when juxtaposed, that the whole shall be uniform in color and finish.

Brise-soleil: A sun-break used in hot climates to shade window openings. Often made-up of horizontal or vertical fins.

Bristol glass: A type of glass made in Bristol, England since 1750, that is very thin and fine. Bristol glassware in blue and milk white is extremely popular.

Brittle: A nonmalleable material such as glass.

Broach: A straight, slender, and pointed object, especially: (A) In ancient English usage, any spire. In local modern English usage, a spire which springs directly from the tower beneath, without any parapet or similar feature at the base. (B) In a lock, the pin over which the barrel of a key fits. (C) A pointed tool for roughly dressing stone.

Broadloom: A term used to denote carpet produced in widths wider than six feet. Was at one time used to identify "high quality." Any carpet manufactured wider than 27 or 36 inches. Simply a designation of width and not a type of weave of carpet.

Brocade: A fabric with a raised embroidered design. The ground is made of silk, satin or velvet.

Brocatelle: Similar to brocade but with a high relief woven design.

Broken measurements: The measuring and noting of individual segments along on side of an area.

Broken pediment: A type of pediment with an apex that is open because the curved lines of scrolls are not connected.

Bronze: An alloy of copper and tin usually in the proportions of about nine parts of copper to one of tin; but the proportions vary, and the metal may still be called bronze if a small amount of lead or zinc enters into it. The term is used also, in combination to give names to many modern alloys in which some other metal takes the place of tin. The analysis of ancient and Oriental bronzes has given some surprising results, showing a much larger proportion of tin; and bell metal, coin metal, and the like, often contain the different ingredients in very different proportions. In architecture, bronze is used in two special ways: first, by the addition to buildings of bronze bas-reliefs or inscribed statues or busts which are not intimately connected with the structure; second, by the use, especially in modern times, of builders' hardware made of bronze instead of iron, brass, or other metal.

Bronze: To give to metal and even to wood or other solid material a specially selected metallic appearance, as of bronze, gold, silver, or the like, by investing its surface with a metal powder , or a liquid, or a paint containing large amounts of metallic powder more or less fine, which being left upon the surface may produce an almost deceptive resemblance to the solid metal. Much the most common use of bronzing is in the imitation of gold or some alloy of gold, and this is improperly called gilding. Gold-bronze powders are made in imitation of red gold, yellow or pure gold, greenish gold, etc., and these are sometimes used together to produce a chromatic effect.

Bronze powder: Metallic used in decorative painting and the like, and by which are produced what is commonly but wrongly called "gilding" in many different tints of gold, and also "silvering," "bronzing," etc.

Bronze-dore: (French) Gilded bronze.

Brussels carpet: A machine-made oriental style carpet.

Brussels lace: A lace made from a net with an applique.

Brussels pitch: 252 or 256 dents per 27 inches in width.

Brussels: A term formerly, but now rarely used to describe a loop pile or round-wire carpet woven on the Wilton loom.

Buckle: To bulge or curve under excessive strain; to deviate from the normal. Used to describe walls and other members which suffer deflection as under extreme load; of metal plates; of boards, and the like, which warp or twist because too thin or light.

Buckles: The same as wrinkles, or other deviations from lying flat, in a carpet.

Bucrane; Bucranium: An ox skull, used as a symbolic decoration in

Roman architecture, in which it had a sacrificial significance, and was confined to altars and temples. It appears to have originated in the primitive practice of affixing the skulls of the oxen sacrificed to the frieze, or other parts, of the temple of the god worship. As a decoration, it was associated with garlands, festoons, and fillets. In Renaissance decoration in Italy it occurs as an arbitrary ornament destitute of particular significance. Its inappropriateness, however, prevented its general adoption.

Buffet: (A) A sideboard; especially a large, stationary, and somewhat elaborate one with shelves, racks, and the like, for serving refreshments. (B) In public places, a room where refreshments are arranged and served from a long counter or table. In both these senses the word has partly lost the original French signification.

Build: To construct or erect a structure by any process of uniting materials or members.

Building system: Means plans, specifications and documentation for a system of manufactured buildings or for a type or a system of building components, which may include structural, electrical, mechanical, plumbing and fire protection systems and other building systems affecting life safety.

Built-ins: Furniture such as, bookcases, cabinets, bars or window seats built into closets or niches.

Built-up level: A floor level elevation change of one or more risers not exceeding four vertical feet.

Bullion fringe: A type of fringe usually found on the bottom of chairs or couch. It is made from twisted corded threads.

Bullnose: An elongated step rounded at one or both side ends of the tread. Also known as a step return.

Bull's Eye Window: A small round window.

Bun foot: A seventeenth century Dutch furniture foot in the shape of a globe or bun.

Bureau: An American style chest of drawers or a French style desk.

Bureau-a-cylindre: (French) Roll-top desk.

Bureau-a-pente: (French) Folding desk with a slant-lid.

Burl: In softwoods, a distortion of the grain due to injury of the tree. In hardwoods, a whorl or twist of the grain near a knot but does not contain a knot. It must have a sound center. The measurement of the burl is the average of the maximum and minimum dimensions of the burl. (A) Very small burl-does not exceed 1/2" in diameter. (B) Small burl-does not exceed 3/4" in diameter. (C) Medium burl-does not exceed 1" in diameter.

Burlap: A course jute or hemp fabric.

Burling: A hand tailoring operation to remove any knots and loose ends, insert missing tufts of surface yarns, and otherwise check the condition of the fabric. Also a repair operation on worn or damaged carpet is reburling.

Butler's pantry: A piece of furniture with drawers or cabinets for dishes and linens usually between the kitchen and the dinning room. It may also be equipped with a counter and a sink.

Butler's tray: An eighteenth century tray devised in Britain with four legs used as a service table.

Butt: The end or back of a member or piece; especially, such part when prepared for another member to butt, or abut against it. Specifically, the larger of the two ends of a log; the back edge of a door; the squared end of a timber prepared for framing and the like. To join squarely, as when two girders meet end to end, forming a Butt Joint.

Butterfly wedge: A piece of wood used to hold together joined boards.

Buy back: To buy back something that one has already sold.

BX cable: A cable comprised of a flexible metallic covering inside of which are two or more insulated wires for carrying electricity.

C

"C" size sheet: Architectural paper size is 24" x 36" and engineering is 22" x 34".

Cabinet: (A) A small cabin, hut, or shelter; hence, (B) A comparatively small room, especially one used by a sovereign or high official for private conferences or interviews. (C) A small closet or piece of furniture provided with shelves, cupboards, or the like, frequently a rich and ornamented piece of furniture of such a character, designed primarily for the safe keeping of valuable articles. (D) A building or part of a building used as in definition C. This usage has become obsolete, but its significance is still seen in the use of the term as signifying a collection of curiosities or works of art.

Cabinet Finish: Interior finish in hard woods, framed, panelled, molded, and varnished or polished like cabinetwork in distinction to finish in soft woods nailed together and commonly painted.

Cabinetmaking: The art and the trade of making fine woodwork, whether for furniture (to which the term was formerly confined) or for the interior finish of houses, ships,

and offices. It is distinguished from the rougher and less elaborate carpenter work by the careful and accurate fitting and high finish which it involves, by the lightness and relatively small scale of its productions, and by its predominant use of fine and hard woods. In carpentry the pieces used are relatively large, and secured by nailing in the majority of cases, while the exterior finish is commonly painted. In cabinetmaking the pieces are small, glue enters largely into the joining of parts, and fine varnishing and polishing are required for the finish.

Cabinet-secretaire: (French) Desk with cabinet above.

Cabinet-vitrine: (French) Cabinet with glass doors.

Cable molding: Molding made in the form of a twisted cord. Common in Romanesque architecture.

Cable: (A) Same as Cable Molding (B) A molding of convex section formed in the flute of a column. It is usual to fill only the lower part of the flute with these cables, that is, for the lower half, or less than half, of the shaft.

Cabriole leg: A furniture leg that curves inward at the foot and outward at the knee in an S-shape. It was popular in Rococo furniture in the seventeenth century.

Cabriolet: (French) Any chair with a concave back.

Cachepot: (French) Porcelain pot used as container.

CAD: Computer Aided Drafting and Design software systems.

Calender: A machine used to give cloth or paper a glossy finish. The material is run through heated rollers thus giving it a smooth appearance.

Calendering: A process of turning thermoplastics into film and sheeting. The plastic is passed between heated rollers and is squeezed into sheets or film.

Calico: A cotton, plain-weave often printed fabric.

Camber: A slight rise or upward curve of an otherwise horizontal, or apparently horizontal, piece or structure. In a steel truss having apparently parallel, horizontal chords, the pieces composing the upper chord are usually made slightly longer between joints than the corresponding parts below; the result being a slight invisible

camber, by which the tendency to sag is overcome. A so-called flat arch is usually built with an intrados having a camber.

Came: A metal strip used in leaded window lights.

Camelback: An English chair or sofa that has a curve or arch in the center.

Cam loom: A loom in which the shedding is performed by means of cams. A velvet loom.

Canape: A French upholstered seat of the eighteenth century also called a settee.

Canape-a-corbeille: (French) Kidney-shaped sofa.

Candela: The unit of measurement of luminous intensity of a light source in a given direction.

Candelabra: Several candles branched out and supported by one stem.

Candlepower: Luminous intensity expressed in candelas.

Canephora: A sculpture of a female carrying a basket on her head.

Canopy: (A) A rooflike structure usually supported on pillars or projecting from a wall, and serving rather a decorative than a protective purpose. It may be movable, as when carried above an important person in a procession, and may consist of an awning of silk or other material supported on poles; or it may be of light material and permanently placed, as above a bedside, whether supported by the posts or hung from the ceiling; or it may be of solid material. In a Gothic niche, the canopy is the most important part. (B) Bed drapery that hangs from posts or the ceiling.

Cant: (A) The angle of inclination of a piece or member to the general surface, especially to the horizontal. (B) A portion or surface which makes an oblique angle with adjoining parts, especially a slope of considerable relative extent.

Cantilever: A member intended to support an overhanging weight, like a bracket; but generally of large size and having a projection much greater than its height; especially, a projecting beam-one which is fixed in a wall or other support at one end, the other end being unsupported. Applied to a bridge or a beam, it means an end projecting beyond the support.

Canvas: Heavy plain-weave cotton or other materials. Used for making tents, awnings, sails, etc.

Cap: The crowning or terminal feature of a vertical member of any structure, either fitting closely upon it or extending somewhat beyond it in horizontal dimensions; thus distinguished from a Finial. The capital of a column, pilaster, or pier, the surbase or cornice-like finish of a pedestal, the cast-iron head of an iron or timber post, the crowning horizontal timber of a stud partition, a timber bolster on a post to diminish the unsupported span of the superstructure, are alike called caps, and the term is also used of a wall coping, door lintel, or handrail as of a balustrade.

Capacitor: An electric energy storage device which when built into or wired to a ballast changes it from low to high power factor.

Cap and band: The covering of a tread and its riser with two separate pieces of carpet.

Capodimonte: A soft paste Italian porcelain with a colored decoration in the center and an ivory background. It was first produced in 1743.

Captain's chair: A chair with vertical spindles forming arms and a heavy railing forming a rounded back. It is a nineteenth century version of the Winsor chair.

Caquetoire or caqueteuse: (French) Conversation chair.

Card table: A small table used for playing games of cards, etc.

Carnauba: A wax that is used in furniture polish. It is made from a Brazilian palm and is very hard.

Carpenter: A worker in wood; especially one who does the larger and rougher work, as of building construction, and as distinguished from a joiner and cabinetmaker.

Carpet: The general term for a soft floor covering fastened to the entire floor from wall to wall.

Carpet cushion: A term used to describe any kind of material placed under carpet to provide softness when it is walked on. Not only does carpet cushion provide a softer feel underfoot, it usually provides added acoustical benefits and longer wear life for the carpet. In some cases the carpet cushion is attached to the carpet when it is manufactured. Also referred to as "lining," "padding" or "underlay," although "carpet cushion" is the preferred term.

Carpet fibers: There are many types of fibers used in the manufacture of carpet. All pile yarns, wool as well as man-made, are spun from staple or short lengths of fiber. Some man-made fibers, however, are also produced in unbroken lengths of continuous filaments. Both types of fibers are often texturized, a process similar to a permanent wave, to impart added bulk. Single strands of either staple or continuous filament fibers are twisted together to form plyed yarns. The yarn fibers are dyed, either before or after they are incorporated into the carpet, by one of the following dyeing methods; stock dyeing, skein dyeing, package dyeing, space dyeing, printing or deep dye printing.

Carpet graphics: Carpet pieces that are used to silence sound and echoes. They are also used in many different colors to make wall murals.

Carpet squares: (Tiles) Loose laid or self-adhesive backed squares of carpet.

Carpet tiles: Tiles that are produced from previously manufactured carpeting of various constructions and backings in sizes that vary anywhere from 12" x 12" to 24" x 24".

The method of their installation is very much like the techniques used for resilient tile although some constructions require specialized methods recommended by their manufacturer.

Carrara glass: Glass that is used for walls and tabletops. It is translucent white and comes from Carrara, Italy.

Cartoon: A drawing or transfer of a drawing upon a large sheet or sheets of paper; especially in Fresco Painting, Fresco Secco, Mural-Painting of other kinds, in Mosaic and in ornamental glass work, the outline in full size more or less filled in with the details of drapery or the like, which is used in the actual preparation of the final painting, mosaic, etc., either by exact copying or by tracing or pouncing. Often used to refer to full-sized paintings used as designs for tapestries.

Cartouche: (A) An ornament which, like an escutcheon, a shield, or an oval or oblong panel, has the central part plain to receive armorial bearings, a cipher, an inscription, or an ornamental or significant piece of painting or sculpture. Frequent in French Renaissance and modern architecture. The term in French denotes such compartments of any shape and filled with any decoration, and is nearly equivalent to Medallion, used in an architectural sense. In English the late neoclassic device of a slightly convex surface, circular or oval in form, is most commonly referred to as a cartouche. (B) An oblong figure with rounded ends, enclosing the hieroglyphics of a royal or divine name, on Egyptian monuments.

Carver chair: A seventeenth century chair that is made from maple or ash with a rush or plank seat. It was named for the first governor of Plymouth colony.

Carving: (A) Cutting in wood, stone, or other resistant material requiring the use of a sharp tool; especially, ornamental cutting, whether in relief or in intaglio. The distinction between carving and sculpture is wholly that of importance and dignity; thus, the figure subjects in Gothic work are hardly ever spoken of as carving, whereas the leaf ornaments in bands and cornices are often so designated. (B) A work or piece of sculpture as described in A.

Caryatid: A column made in the form of a female figure. Columns or pilasters carved all or partially as human figures.

Case: (A) A box, enclosure, or hollow receptacle, as the space in which a stairway is built: a staircase. (B) Same as Casing. (C) The carcass of structural framework of a house

or other building. (Rare in United States.)

Case, door: A frame consisting of jamb pieces and lintel or head framed or nailed together, to one side of which the door is hung, and in which it closes; that face of the frame or case having a rebate so that the door when closed into the rebate shall be flush with the wall, or in a plane parallel with the face of the wall. In thin walls and partitions the case is as thick as the partition, and finished with a trim on either side the latter. In thick walls the case finishes with a trim on one side, and a bead or molding against the masonry or plastered jam on the other.

Casein painting: Painting with the use of casein, one of the constituents of milk, which combines chemically with quicklime. This combination can be diluted with water, and, when dry, is very hard and insoluble. It follows, then, that this medium can be employed on freshly plastered walls. It can also be used on dry plaster. Casein is prepared from cheese by trituration, but even fresh white cheese may be used instead of pure casein without further treatment. To prepare the pigments, first stir up three parts of cheese and one of fat slaked lime.

The quantity of color to be added must be learned by experience. Earth colors and metallic oxides should be used, and for white, oxide of zinc or sulfite of baryta, or whiting. The medium must be freshly prepared every day, and this is probably the reason why the use of it is infrequent. Even the small amount of casein to be found in milk unmixed with quicklime makes it an excellent medium, more or less insoluble. The Italians use it as a medium both on fresh and dry plaster, preferably on the former.

Casement: (A) A window having hinged or pivoted sash, opening either outward or inward. In northern Germany many such windows open outward, and this is preferred, except where it is desired to put up secondary or outer fixed sash (forming "double windows") in winter. English country houses were commonly fitted with light iron sash in very small casements. These also opened outward, and were held by long hooks or some other form of sash-holder. (B) One leaf or swinging frame forming part of such a window, and thus in British usage distinguished from a sash. In the United States, usually called casement sash. (C) In medieval architecture, a deep,

hollow molding similar to the Scotia of classic architecture.

Casement cloth: Any plain loosely-woven or semi-sheer drapery fabric.

Casework: All the parts that constitute a finished case or cabinet, inclusive of doors, drawers, and shelves.

Cast: A reproduction of the forms of any object, usually in a soft material which will harden after a time. The cast first taken, as of a bas-relief, a molding, or the like, is usually called the mold; and is, of course, the reverse of the original. That which is taken from the mold will be an exact copy of the original object. It is common to make casts in plaster and in sulphur, the latter having the great advantage that it does not shrink in setting; and molds of bas-reliefs and the like are made of gelatine, which is capable of easy manipulation. The second cast, or reproduction of the original object, is most commonly of Plaster of Paris.

Caster: A wheel placed on the bottom of furniture enabling it to be rolled rather than carried.

Casting: (A) The art and act of making casts. (B) Anything cast, whether of metal or other material, which has been melted and run into a mold; or of plaster, cement, or the like, mixed with water, which has been allowed to set in a mold. Castings of bronze, brass, and zinc and the like are much used in the industrial arts, cast bronze having been particularly the metal for fine art objects in use from time immemorial. It is usual to finish castings after they leave the mold; and this is done with fine tools, files, and the like, and should be done by the artist himself who has made the original model. When a mold is made for casting, it must be so shaped that the hardened metal or other substance will leave the mold rightly, and will not tear it by breaking its particles away. For this reason the forms which are capable of being produced in an original casting are limited in their character, and the design for a casting must be different from that which is to be wrought by hammered work or in other ways. On these accounts, cast iron, being much too hard for successful finishing by hand, is hardly fit for delicate ornamentation; and yet the Berlin iron work, originating in a patriotic movement in 1813, has much charm. Medals of bronze, silver, and the like are more often struck by a die, but are sometimes cast; and the beautiful large metals (medallions) of the Renaissance are generally cast bas-reliefs of bronze. (C) A method of

turning thermoplastics into sheeting, film, and rigid sheets. The material is heated into a fluid, poured into a mold and cured and is then removed from the mold.

Cast iron: Iron which is shaped by being run into a mold while melted, as described under casting. In ordinary commercial usage a compound of iron and carbon; the material which runs directly in liquid form from the blast furnace, and which hardens in the mold. From cast iron is made the purer iron which is used for working with the hammer, and also steel. Cast iron is brittle and hard, and is not capable of being welded, that is to say, of having two parts united when hammered together while hot, the property in iron which is most important to it as a material for decoration.

Catch: A contrivance for automatically securing a door, shutter, or a similar movable leaf by the action of gravity or of a spring. In some of its more elaborate forms hardly to be distinguished from a latch or spring lock.

Cathedral: (more properly cathedral church). The church in which is set up the bishop's Throne or Cathedra. This church may be considered as the bishop's throne room; or, if the choir be considered as the throne room, then the cathedral with chapter house and other accessories, and the actual residence of the bishop, together with the cloisters and other enclosed spaces, may be considered as the episcopal palace, resembling a royal or grand ducal palace in having rooms for business and ceremony combined in the same building with the residence of the prince and his officers and attendants. The cathedral itself is not necessarily large nor splendid, nor is there any architectural style or character which can be said to belong to it in a peculiar sense. In Athens, the Old Cathedral, which was used without interruption until the middle of the present century, remains one of the smallest churches in the world, and capable of containing a congregation of only a few score.

Caulking: (A) The act or method of securing the end of a timber, like a girder or tie beam, to another on which it rests at right angles (as the wall plate or sill) by means of a cog hold. (B) The operation or method of rendering a joint tight, as against water or gas, by driving into its interstices with a chisel or other tool some plastic or elastic substance, such as oakum and tar in the decks

of ships, lead in the hubs of soil pipes, etc. (C) In boiler work and hydraulic work a process for making a joint stream or water tight by upsetting the edges of the steel or iron plates. (Written also Calking, Caulking, Cocking, Cogging.)

Caulking compound: An adhesive that bends easily and is used to fill in cracks.

Cavetto molding: Hollow molding with a quarter circle section.

Cavity ratio: A number indicating cavity proportions calculated from length, width and height.

Cedar: A red wood with a fragrance that protects clothing from moths.

Ceiling: (A) The covering of a wall surface, especially on the interior; or of the under side of a floor; the material used being always supposed to be a simple and ordinary one. Thus, ceiling is of thin boards or of lath and plaster, but never of tile, nor is the term applied to the surface afforded by the solid material of a wall or floor; except as under B. (B) By extension from A, the under side of a floor which provides the roofing or enclosure at top of a room or other space below. In this case, it is the surface alone which is designated without reference to material.

Ceiling cavity ratio: A numerical relationship of the vertical distance between luminaire mounting height and ceiling height to room width and length. It is used with the Zonal Cavity method of calculating average illumination levels.

Ceiling outlet: An air diffuser mounted in the ceiling.

Celadon: A putty to sea-green colored glaze used on Chinese stoneware.

Celature: The art of decorating metals by chasing, engraving, or repousse work.

Cellar: (A) The space below the ground story or the basement story of a building, enclosed by the foundation walls, and therefore wholly, or almost entirely, below the surface of the surrounding ground. The distinction between cellar and basement story is not absolute, and, in some cases, may depend on the use to which such a space is put, as much as on its relative situation. Thus, in an English-basement house, the front portion of the lowest, nearly subterranean, story will frequently be without windows, and used merely for storage of fuel and the like, and will therefore be referred to as a cellar; but the same story might be equally well provided with large windows opening into an area, and would then be used as a living room or for domestic offices, and would be called a basement story. Hence, as such a space is commonly used for storage and the like, (B) Any underground or partly underground place of deposit for wine, provisions, fuel, or the like.

Cellar, wine: A room arranged for the reception of wine and other fermented or distilled liquors. The primary requisite is that it should have a very even temperature, the warmth of the atmosphere within it changing gradually, if at all. Ventilation is only needed so far as dampness is to be avoided, and a very slow changing of the air should be sufficient for this. Excellent results have followed, when the general cellar space is dry, but shutting off a piece of it completely without any provision whatever for the changing of air. It is customary to provide a separate room for wine, etc., in casks and for that which is bottled. The cellar for bottled liquors should be fitted up with shelves, although devices of light ironwork, wire, etc., and also of baked clay in the form of hollow tiles, have been made for the same purpose. With ordinary wooden shelving, a distinction must be made between bottles that are to set up and those which are to be laid on their sides; for these latter it is good to arrange the shelving so as to make diagonal compartments like very large pigeonholes set cornerwise, with one of the angles pointing downward.

Cellaret: A small chest used to cool and store wine made from wood and lined with lead.

Cellular carrying capacity: The capacity for wire is determined by the safest operating temperature.

Cellulose: A carbohydrate of complex molecular structure which forms the basic framework of plant cells and walls. Used as a basic raw material in making rayon.

Cement: (A) Any of various calcined mixtures of limestone and clay, water and sand used to form concrete. (B) A soft sticky substance that dries hard and is used to mend broken objects or to make things adhere. (C) To secure together by means of cement. (D) A plastic roofing material made of broken slate mixed with tar, asphalt, or some similar material.

Center drawer guide: Wooden tracking placed under a drawer to allow it to open easily.

Center Mold: A thin piece of board or the like, the edge of which is shaped to a given profile, and which, when rotated about a pivot at one end, will cut corresponding circular moldings in soft plaster or the like.

Center of view: The point where the observer point is projected into the picture plane.

Centrally planned: A building planned to radiate from a central point in contrast to axial plan.

Ceramics: (A) The art and industry of making objects of baked clay. (B) Objects made of baked clay taken collectively. The arts of baked clay applicable to architecture are of two sorts; in one the clay surface, whether flat or modelled, is left without glaze or polish of any kind. In the other, which forms the subject of the present article, the processes of the potter are employed. The most common forms of earthenware in use in architecture are floor, roof, and wall tiling, the last having for its primary object the protection of buildings by an indestructible surface, capable of resisting the effects of weather and changes of temperature. The glazed or enamelled face which offers most opportunity for the characteristic colors of pottery in decoration is less durable under friction than bodies of a semivitreous fracture (such as porcelain or stoneware), and consequently less adapted for floor tiling than for walls or roofs. When an ordinary earthenware body is used for this purpose, the floor is slippery so long as the glaze retains its freshness, and as soon as it is worn down by use the soft substratum offers little resistance, and its decoration is quickly destroyed. The majolica pavements of the Italian Cinquecento offer extreme instances of this, as in the floor of Raphael's Loggia in the Vatican, and the church of S. Maria del Popolo in Rome, as also in churches at Bologna, Parma, Venice, and Siena, dating from 1480 onwards. The floor tiles depending for hardness on a glazed surface that

have stood the test of time best are those made on the Spanish or Spanish-Moorish system, in which compartments are filled in with thick colored glazes, just as the enamel fills the compartments of Cloisonne ware. These tiles of the sixteenth and seventeenth centuries were an article of export, as we find them in Italy, especially in Genoa, and elsewhere. The tiles in the Mayor's chapel at Bristol are of this class. In the medieval floor tile the soft lead glazes have disappeared, except in very sheltered positions, leaving the incised patterns exposed to the wear of feet, so that in many cases only the harder clay is left. Tiles of this class have been called Norman tiles, as they are more frequent in Normandy than elsewhere, and of much earlier date. The earliest known, probably, are those from the palace of the dukes of Normandy, built within the precinct of the abbey of S. Etienne at Caen, and in England those from Castle Acre, Norfolk, of about the end of the thirteenth century. There is a very fine example in the chapter house at Westminster, probably of a rather later date. The practice of inlaying patterns (of which the foregoing are instances) is of a very great antiquity, as Egyptian examples exist of 1200 B.C. in which the colored glass, sometimes called porcelain, forms an inlaid pattern.

Certosina: A technique in which light materials are inlaid into a dark background. Ornate designs made from ivory, light wood, and bone are used.

Chain: (A) The binder warp yarn that works over and under the filling shots of the carpet. (B) Axminster loom refers to the endless chain that carries the tube frames. (C) Dobby loom refers to the endless chain of pattern selector bars.

Chain binders: Those yarns in woven carpets that run alternately over and under the weft and filling yarns in a lengthwise direction to bind all the construction yarns together.

Chairbound: A person who is confined to or needs to use a wheelchair during the working day.

Chair rail: A horizontal band or strip, generally of wood, secured to the sides of a room at a height from the floor equivalent to the usual height of the backs of chairs, in order to prevent them from injuring the face of the wall. It is commonly decoratively treated to conform with the general woodwork, and the

space of wall beneath is often finished as a dado.

Chaise: (French) Side chair.

Chaise-a-capucine: (French) Low slipper chair.

Chaise-brisee: (French) Chaise-longue with two parts).

Chalk board: A surface that can be written on, usually with chalk.

Chalking: Powdering of the paint film on the film surface. Mild chalking can be desirable however heavy chalking should be removed prior to repainting.

Chamfer: The bevel or oblique surface produced by cutting away a corner or arris. When the chamfer does not extend the whole length of the arris, it is called a stopped chamfer. When instead of a bevel there is a concave surface replacing the arris, it is called a concave chamfer. A beaded chamfer is one in which a convex bead is left projecting from the bevel of the chamfer. A beaded chamfer is one in which a convex bead is left projecting from the bevel of the chamfer. Chamfers occur principally in woodwork, and occasionally in stone cutting.

Chandelier: (French) Hanging lighting fixture.

Channeled or fluted back: Upholstered back with rows of vertical fabric channels.

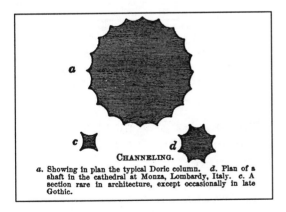

CHANNELING.

a. Showing in plan the typical Doric column. *d.* Plan of a shaft in the cathedral at Monza, Lombardy, Italy. *c.* A section rare in architecture, except occasionally in late Gothic.

Channeling: The breaking up of a surface by means of channels or grooves, usually near together and parallel; channels collectively.

Chase: A groove or channel formed in a structure, as in the face of a wall, to receive some accessory such as flues, wires, sliding weights, or the like. A chase may be left in a wall for the future joining to it of an abutting wall to be built later. A chase differs from a groove mainly in being relatively large, and in not ordinarily calling for accurate fitting to whatever it is to receive.

Chattily: A factory which produces opaque porcelain. It was founded in Chattily, France in 1725.

Check: A crack or split caused by the uneven shrinkage of wood while seasoning or drying. It is to guard against checks that lumber is quarter sawed, and large sticks, especially posts, have their hearts bored out.

Checker: (A) Any decoration which divides a surface into equal squares treated alternately in different ways, as with different colors or with high and low relief. (B) A form of ornament in which the compartments are uniformly square, as in late Romanesque and in Gothic surface carving. (C) With the article, one of the squares in checker work.

Checker-work: Decoration in the form of a checker or chess board. Made up of contrasting square or rectangular pieces or pavers.

Chelsea porcelain: A porcelain made in England and originally made with tin oxide. It has a soft paste and often copies Meissen.

Chene: (French) Oak.

Chenets: (French) Andirons.

Chenille: A pile fabric woven by the insertion of a prepared weft row of surface yarn tufts in a "fur" or "caterpillar" form through very fine but strong cotton "catcher" warp yarns, and over a heavy woolen backing yarn.

Cherry: A wood that is pale brown in color but darkens with age. It carves well and has a fine grain.

Cherub: (A) A symbolic, or allegorical decoration consisting of an infant's head with wings, common in late Italian seventeenth-century carving, and on English and American tombstones of the seventeenth and eighteenth centuries. (B) In the art of the sixteenth century and later, a naked child in any religious or liturgical representation. These figures are not often winged. (C) In ancient Jewish

and in Byzantine art a symbolic figure with six wings, as on the Ark in Solomon's Temple, and on the pendentives of Hagia Sophia, Constantinople.

Chestnut: A hard wood reddish-brown in color, often used for inlay.

Chest of drawers: A wooden case with drawers; also a large commode.

Chest-on-chest: One chest of drawers sitting on top of another larger one.

Cheval glass: A mirror which stands on splayed feet, pivots from posts and is full length in size.

Chevet: (French) Bedside.

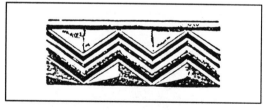

Chevron: A zigzag molding. Common in Romanesque architecture.

Chiaroscuro: Painting technique using shade and lighting.

Chiffonier: (French) Chest of drawers. A cabinet with drawers and usually a mirror.

Chimney: That part of a building which contains a flue or flues for conveying smoke or the like to the outer air, and often encloses also the fireplace, if there is one; specifically, that portion which rises above the roof.

China: Porcelain which was first made in China.

China cabinet: A cabinet with doors and shelves in which dishes are stored.

Chinoiserie: (French) Chinese style of cloth, wallpaper and furniture popular in the seventeenth and eighteenth century.

Chipolin painting: The imitation in painting of cipolino marble; hence, of any marble of light gray or greenish veins.

Chord: (A) In geometry, the straight line drawn between the extremities of an arc. (B) One of the two principal members extending along the top and bottom of a truss.

Chrome: A bright metallic coating applied to steel and other metals to protect it from oxidation.

Churrigueresque: Spanish and Latin Baroque architecture characterized by extreme and fancy detail.

Cinnabar lacquer: Lacquer which has been colored with a red sulfide containing mercury.

Circa: About or approximate date.

Circuit breaker: Resettable safety device to prevent excess current flow.

Ciseleur: (French) A craftsman who decorates metals by chiselling. A chiseller.

Cladding: The external skin of a structure applied for both aesthetics and protection.

Clamp: A piece or instrument for securing or holding, generally distinguished from other devices used for that purpose as being applied to the surface of the parts, and not passing through the material, although perhaps entering a short distance. It may be a member to unite two or more parts of a structure permanently together, as a cleat or strap; or a tool to hold temporarily one or more pieces of material in process of being prepared or finished, as a carpenter's screw clamp.

Clamp down metal moldings: Also known in the industry as "tap down". Commercially available in metal or metal with a vinyl covering. Used to protect a carpet edge from unraveling or wear.

Class P ballast: Contains a thermal protective device which deactivates the ballast when the case reaches a certain critical temperature. The device resets automatically when the case temperature drops to a lower temperature.

Clavichord: A medieval instrument similar in appearance to a spinet piano.

Claw-and-ball foot: A carved animal or bird foot which holds a ball. Popular in the eighteenth century.

Clear: (A) Open, free of obstruction. (B) Clean, without impurities or defects; without admixture. Thus, clear cement is cement unmixed with sand or lime. (C) In connection with lumber, free from knots, shakes, sap, and the like. (D) Unobstructed space; opening considered as between the inside limits of two opposite parts. Chiefly used in the adjectival phase, in the clear-i.e. taken or measured at the narrowest part of an opening; in general, the shortest or perpendicular distance so taken.

Clear finish: A transparent coating or paint.

Cleat: (A) A strip of wood nailed, screwed, or otherwise fastened across a number of boards to hold them together or to stiffen or otherwise strengthen them; or secured to a wall or other upright as a support for a shelf, or the like. The cleat differs from the batten generally in being smaller and in having only the significance of a piece used to secure together planks or boards laid edge to edge, or of stiffening a very wide piece of plank or board. The common term Batten Door would be better described as Cleat Door, for the transverse piece is short and need not be hereby; it may be thought, however, that the battens referred to in this term are the longitudinal or principal pieces. (B) A device for temporarily attaching a cord, as of an awning; usually of metal and consisting of a shank or short leg from which two arms extend in opposite directions. The cleat being secured in place by the shank, the cord may be wound about the arms.

Clerestory: That part of a building which rises above roofs of other parts, and which has windows in its walls. The term is especially used for medieval churches, whose division into a central nave and side aisles of less width and height made the opening up of the wider central nave a natural and obvious arrangement. It dates back, therefore, at least as far as the earliest Christian basilicas. A similar arrangement is, however, traceable in some buildings of Roman antiquity.

Clichy: A suburb of Paris which is well known for its paperweights.

Clinch: To bend over and hammer down the protruding point of a nail so that it cannot be withdrawn; to secure or fasten a nailed structure by so doing.

Closed construction: That condition when any building, component, assembly, subassembly, or system is manufactured in such a manner that all portions cannot be readily inspected at the installation site without disassembly or destruction thereof.

Closed step: Steps ending at each end at a wall.

Closed system: A system made up of components and subsections that are related in dimension.

Closet: (A) Originally, a private room; the sitting room or chamber of a person of some distinction. (B) In modern usage, a place for storage, distinguished from a cupboard only as being larger, perhaps large enough for a person to enter. By extension, the term covers such a small room when fitted with conveniences for washing, and the like, as a wash closet, a dressing closet.

Closet, plate: In Great Britain, a closet or small room connected with the butler's offices for the custody of plate. When the plate is of much value, such a closet is commonly made fireproof and is called a plate room or plate safe. In the United States, it is usually a much less pretentious compartment called a silver closet or silver safe.

Cloth-backed: A wallcovering which has a backing of woven or knitted yarns.

Clothes press: A sixteenth century cabinet used to hang clothes.

Cloth of gold: Gold and silver woven into a web of silk cloth.

Coalport: English ceramics. Also a factory where eighteenth century Sevres is reproduced.

Coat: A layer of paint, plaster, mortar, or the like as applied to a wall or floor. The term is restricted to a liquid or semiliquid substance so applied.

Coating adhesion: A measure of the strength of the bond between the surface coating and the substratum or backing of a wallcovering.

Cobbler's bench: A bench used by shoemakers with compartments built in for tools.

Cock, bibb: (Sometimes abbreviated "bibb.") A fitting for the discharge of water into fixtures, usually with a bent down nozzle.

Cockling: A curliness or crimpiness appearing in the cut face pile as a result of a yarn condition.

Cocoa matting: A doormat made with coconut fiber.

Coefficient of Utilization: (CU) A ratio representing the portion of light emitted by a luminaire in any particular installation that actually gets down to the work plane. The coefficient of utilization thus indicates the combined efficiency of the luminaire, room proportions and room finish reflectances. The ratio of the luminous flux (lumens) from a luminaire is calculated as received on the work-plane to the luminous flux emitted by the luminaires lamps alone.

Coffre: (French) Chest.

Coiffeuse: (French) A nineteenth century French dressing table.

Cold cathode lamp: An electric-discharge lamp whose mode of operation is that of a glow discharge.

Color and sample boards: Presentation aids used in interior design to show samples.

Color flag: A total color line clipped together.

Color Rendering Index: (CRI) Measure of the degree of color shift objects undergo when illuminated by the light source as compared with the color of those same objects when illuminated by a reference source of comparable color temperature.

Color temperature: The absolute temperature of a blackbody radiator having a chromaticity equal to that of the light source.

Column: (A) A pillar or post; a slender pier especially one that carries a weight and acts as an upright supporting member. In this general sense, the word has been applied to the supporting parts of iron frames of all sorts; so that where the uprights of a piece of carpentry work would commonly be called posts, the cast-iron or wrought-iron uprights are called columns. (B) In special architectural sense, a supporting member of stone or some material used in close imitation of stone and composed of three parts; capital, shaft, and base; the shaft, moreover, being either cylindrical or approximately so,-that is, a many-sided prism, or a reeded or fluted body whose general shape is cylindrical. In this sense a column need not carry a weight at all large in proportion to its mass; thus the decorative use of columns for memorial purposes involves the placing of a statue, a bust, a globe, a vase, or similar object, slight in proportion to the column itself, as the only weight superimposed upon the capital. The term is still employed where some of the above characteristics do not exist; thus, in the earliest columnar architecture, that of the Egyptians, there is no base, and the earliest columnar structures of the Greeks, namely those of the Doric order, were also without bases. Capitals are, however, universal, and are to be considered as mainly decorative in character.

Comb-back chair: A chair that has spindles on the back which resemble a comb.

Combination: A term which refers to yarns or fabrics; (A) A combination yarn is composed of two or more yarns having the same or different fibers or twists; e.g., one yarn may have a high twist; the other, little or no twist. (B) A combination fabric is one which uses the above yarns.

Commemorative wallpaper or fabric: Wallpaper or fabric designs which celebrate a historic person or event.

Commercial matching: Matching of colors within acceptable tolerances, or with a color variation that is barely detectable to the naked eye.

Commode: (French) Low chest of drawers. A decorative chest of drawers.

Communication and identification system: Standardized signs used to identify circulation routes, and hazards for physically handicapped people.

Companion fabric or wallpaper: Material designed to be used with another similar design in the same room.

Compatible for color and grain: For purposes of millwork, this phrase means that members shall be selected so that lighter than average color members will not be adjacent to darker than average color members, and there will be no sharp contrast in color between the adjacent members. Two adjacent members shall not be widely dissimilar in grain, character and figure.

Composition: (I.) (A) In fine art, the act of arranging parts in a design; the term being equally applicable to color taken by itself, or to line taken by itself, or to masses of light and shade, or to all the elements of the work of art considered as making up the general result. Also, the act of making such arrangements in design. (B) A design, considered as the result of several or many parts or elements combined into one.

Composition: (II.) A material made up artificially and used in modeling decorative friezes, centerpieces, and the like; a general term used for plastic material of unknown or unspecified make.

Compotier: (French) Container for stewed fruit, jellies, jams, etc.

Compressed edge technique: A method of anchoring edges of carpet on the tackless strips while installing wall to wall carpeting.

Compressed seam technique: An installation technique used to complete the formation of a durable and almost inconspicuous seam in two pieces of carpet being glued down to the floor.

Compression molding: Heat is applied to thermosetting materials and squeezed into desired shape. This process is not usually done on thermoplastic.

Cone of vision: The angle that encompasses the view of the observer, usually 45°-60°. The important elements of the drawing should be within this cone of vision.

Cone reflector: Parabolic reflector that directs light downward thereby eliminating brightness at high angles.

Console: (French) Wall table. A decorative bracket with a compound curved outline, the height is usually larger than the projection. A projecting, scroll-shaped member, usually understood as being a variety of corbel or bracket, but having always parallel, nearly plane sides. It is commonly altogether decorative in its purpose, as a scroll-shaped figure used to support a window head, a table top, or the like. The definition is generally taken as a bracket which has a height at least twice as great as its projection; and the term cantilever or modillion is supposed to be more appropriate for a bracket or corbel which projects more in proportion. But these definitions are all vague; and the console is usually an ornamental bracket whose sides are parallel and with those sides ornamental with scrolls.

Console table: A table usually made of wood or marble that stands against a wall.

Console-desserte: (French) Serving table.

Construction, general: (A) The manner in which anything is composed or put together. (B) The act and the art of putting parts together to produce a whole. (C) a completed piece of work of a somewhat elaborate kind; especially a building in the ordinary sense.

Construction, carpet: Carpet construction is defined by stating the manufacturing method (tufted, woven, etc.), and the final arrangement of materials achieved by following specifications.

Consultation: The process of consulting a professional interior designer for advice on the design and decoration of a room, space or building interior, including colors, fabrics, styles and selection of furnishings and accessories, layout and planning.

Continuous filament: Continuous strand of synthetic fiber extruded in yarn form, without the need for spinning which all natural fibers require.

Contrast: The difference in brightness (luminance) of an object and its background.

Contrast Rendition Factor (CRF): The ratio of visual task contrast with a given lighting environment to the contrast with sphere illumination. Contrast measured under sphere illumination is defined as 1.00.

Conversation pit: A sunken area of a room with furniture.

Converter: A fabric company that does its own processing.

Convertible sofa: An upholstered sofa that converts into a full-size bed.

Cool beam lamps: Incandescent PAR lamps that use a special coating (dichronic interference filter) on the reflectorized portion of the bulb to allow heat to pass out the back while reflecting only visible energy to the task, thereby providing a "cool beam" of light.

Cope: To overhang with a downward slope, as the soffit of a corona. Generally, cope over.

Coped: To cut the end of one member to match the profile of another molded member.

Coping: Material or a member used to form a capping or finish at the top of a wall, pier, or the like to protect it by throwing off the water on one or both sides. In some cases a level coping suffices, if of stones or tiles wider than the walls; usually it is formed with a pitch one way or from the center both ways. The medieval architects gave great attention to their copings, especially on gable walls, which were commonly carried above the roof, and on balustrades and parapets, finishing them usually with a roll or astragal on top, a slope each way, sometimes in steps, and a throating or grooving on the under edge where it projected beyond the wall. Wooden or metal copings are employed over fences and in cheap construction.

Coquillage: A rococo decoration in the form of scallop shells.

Cork: The outer bark of a Mediterranean oak tree used for wall coverings and insulation.

Corner block: A block used to strengthen chair rails or cabinets.

Corner chair: A chair that has a diagonal seat and high arms popular in the eighteenth century.

Corner cupboard: A triangular cupboard that either hangs or stands on three feet. It fits into a corner of a room and often is used to hold china.

Cornice: The crowning member of a wall; or part of a wall; as a coping or water table treated architecturally. It has several special meanings. (A) In the classical entablature, the uppermost of its three principal members. It may crown a colonnade, a dado or basement wall, a porch, or even a purely ornamental feature, like the casing of a window. In buildings of classical design having more than one story, a cornice crowns the whole wall, and is proportioned rather to the height of that wall than to the height of the uppermost order if the building is of columnar architecture. In this sense the wall cornice has been said to have been borrowed from the order. (B) In architecture other than Greco-Roman and its imitations, the uppermost feature of a wall of masonry. Thus, the cornice of many Romanesque churches consists of a slab of stone projecting a few inches from the face of a wall, and supported, or apparently supported, where it overhangs, by corbels. Such a cornice may or may not carry a gutter. In some cases a row of small arches (a blind arcade) is formed under the top of the wall, and seems to carry the projecting stone. In the fully developed Gothic style the cornice generally consists of three members: first and lowest, a sculptured band; second, a drip molding of considerable projection, the hollow beneath which is apt to be dwelt upon as forming an effective line of shadow; third, the steeply inclined weathering above, which is continued either to the gutter or is carried up so high as to form the face of the gutter cut in the stone behind it, or which carries a parapet of some sort. In wooden buildings there is confusion between B and C. (C) So much of the roof as projects beyond the face of the wall and affords shelter to the uppermost windows, besides giving shadow. It is the eaves treated in a decorative way. B is often called Wall Cornice. C is called also Roof Cornice. It is to be observed that when the uppermost courses of the main wall have no projection, or very little, it is common to say that the building has no cornice. Thus, the Ducal Palace of Venice has on its two principal fronts a course of marble decorated with a cove, a fillet, and a bead, but not more than four courses of brick in total height and having no more than 7 inches projection, although at least 85 feet above the pavement of the square; but this slight coping carries a series of battlement-like upright ornaments of marble 7 feet high. In some high modern buildings with flat roofs, the cornice has been treated in a similar manner, and a parapet replaces its projection so far as architectural effect is concerned. By extension, the term applies to a similar decorative member of whatever material, similarly placed, as at the top of a piece of furniture, of an interior wall or partition, or the like. Thus, cornices in the interiors of houses are usually formed of a series of plaster moldings. (D) A piece of light woodwork, embossed metal, or the like, which is set horizontally at the top of a window casing within, either to conceal the rod and rings which carry the curtains, or to form a lambrequin as part of the upholstery, or to give emphasis to the height of the window. In this sense, the term is allied with the Italian use of the same word for a frame, as of a picture, a bas-relief, or the like.

Cornice or cove lighting: Lighting fixtures hidden in a wall or ceiling by a cornice.

Cornucopia: A horn of plenty filled with fruits and vegetables used for decoration.

Corridor lobby: A wheelchair turnaround space in a corridor provided with seating.

Corridor rest stops: Wheelchair parking and seating provided at intervals in a corridor.

Corrosion: The process of gradual decomposition or wearing away by chemical action, as by the action of water on iron, producing rust. Differing from disintegration, which is the result of mechanical action. In practice, the term is generally used only in the case of metals, decay being the usual term in the case of stone or wood.

Cotton: (A) A soft, white, fibrous substance composed of the hairs clothing the seeds of an erect, freely branching tropical plant (cotton plant). (B) Fabric made from the natural vegetable fiber cotton.

Count: (A) A number identifying yarn size or weight per unit length or vice versa, depending on the particular system being used. (B) Count of fabric is indicated by the number of warp ends and filling ends per inch.

Counter ceiling: A secondary ceiling interposed between the floor and ceiling of a room, to exclude sounds originating in the room above. A layer of sound-obstructing material or deafening, either mineral wool, sawdust, or the like, is sometimes spread over the upper surface of the counter ceiling to assist in opposing the transmission of sound.

Countersink: (A) A hole or depression made by or for countersinking. In this sense, also countersinking. (B) An instrument for countersinking. (C) To form a depression or hole for the reception of a piece or member which is not to project beyond the general surface. The cutting may be made to fit accurately the object, as in setting a hinge flush with the surrounding woodwork, or it may be a recess larger than the member, as a hole made to receive the head of a bolt.

(D) To let into a surface by means of a recess as above described.

Cover: Descriptive of how the underlying structure is concealed by the face yarn.

Coverlet: A crocheted or handwoven bedspread.

Crab: A hand device usually used for stretching carpet in a small area where a power stretcher or knee kicker cannot be used.

Cramp: (A) In masonry, a small metal member to secure together two adjoining parts or pieces. It is usually a short flat bar, having its two ends turned down at right angles and embedded in holes in the stones. (B) Same as Clamp.

Cranberry glass: A glass used for vases and glasses that is clear and light red.

Crazing: Fine cracks that appear together on the surface of cement or on ceramics.

Credenza: A buffet with lion style feet, doors and drawers from the Renaissance era.

Creel: The rack located adjacent to a tufting machine which holds the cones of pile yarn which supply yarn to the needles of a tufting machine.

Creeling: The process of mounting yarn packages on the yarn package holder in the creel.

Cremaillere: (French) Hearth.

Crest, cresting: An ornamental member, or a group or series of members, used to form a decorative finish at the top of any structure; as along the ridge of a roof, as an elaborate coping, the top of a pinnacle, or the like. Crest may perhaps be considered as restricted to mean an isolated single ornament, while cresting may be more properly applied to a continuous feature.

Crewel work: Embroidery that originates from the Jacobean period and is usually done on linen.

Crimp: In fiber, a nonlinear configuration, such as a sawtooth, zig-zag or random curl relative to the fiber axis. In woven fabrics, nonlinear yarn configurations caused by three-dimensional displacements such as the zig-zagging of warp yarn over fill yarn. Most synthetic fibers, both staple and filament, used in carpets are crimped. Fiber crimp increases bulk and cover and facilitates

interlocking of staple fibers in spun yarns.

Crocket: A decorative carved terminal of a spire or gable. Common in Gothic architecture.

Crocking: Term used to describe excess color rubbing off as the result of improper dye penetration, fixation, or selection.

Croft: An eighteenth century and nineteenth century cabinet used for writing or filling.

Crook: A deviation edgewise from a straight line drawn from end to end of a piece. It is measured at the point of greatest distance from the straight line.

Cropping: The passage of carpet under a revolving cylinder fitted with cutting blades to obtain a level surface and a uniform height of pile.

Crossbanding: In the construction of flush doors, the veneer which is placed between the core and face veneers with the direction of the grain at right angles to that of the face veneer.

Cross bracing: (A) Any system of bracing with crossed struts or ties, as in many bridge trusses. (B) In house carpentry, the term is used specifically for continuous lines of crossed braces or struts between the floor joists, these lines of cross bracing being put in at intervals of 6 or 8 feet to stiffen the floors by distributing over several joists any shock or strain upon one. Generally called Bridging, and Cross Bridging or Herringbone Bridging.

Cross dyed: Multicolored effects produced in a fabric with fibers of different dye affinities.

Cross light: (A) Light received from windows in walls at right angles to each other and so distinguished from Counter light from windows in opposite walls. (B) The same as Counter light. Restriction to the first sense is more scientific. In this sense cross light is permissible from the side and front.

Crossgrained: Having the grain transverse or oblique to the length; used particularly of boards in which, owing to the crookedness of the log from which they are cut, the grain lies diagonally or crooked in the plane or in the width of the board, such stuff being liable to chip under the plane, and difficult to work.

Cross section: A view of an object that cuts through at its longest axis from a right angle.

Cross stretcher: A brace in the shape of a letter X used to join chair legs.

Crystal: Glass which contains a large quantity of lead, extremely lustrous, and when tapped will ring.

Cubic foot: Measuring unit. Water is measured by gallons and cement is measured by pounds.

Cul-de-lampe: A conical ornamental support.

Cup: A deviation in the face of a piece from a straight line drawn from edge to edge of a piece. It is measured at the point of greatest distance from the straight line.

Cupboard: Originally a set of shelves upon which dishes, silver plate, and the like could be displayed; by transition, and as the decorative piece of furniture in question has disappeared from use, a small and shallow closet.

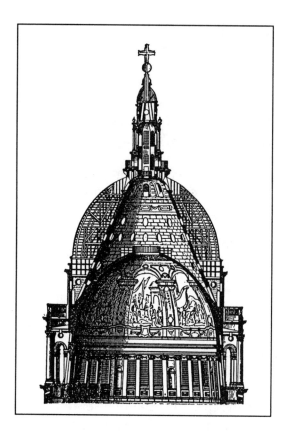

Cupola: A bowl-shaped vault; and the imitation of such a vault in lighter materials.

Curf: An incision, groove, or cut made by a saw or other cutting tool, especially one across the width of a board or molding, usually for the purpose of facilitating its being bent to a curve. Chimneys and piers which have leaned from the vertical are sometimes restored to verticality by cutting a curf in the side from which they lean. In shaping a square timber from the log by hewing, it is common first to cut along one side of the log a series of curfs; that is, notches, the depth of which is regulated so as to form a gauge for the subsequent cutting away of the wood between.

Curio cabinet: see vitrine.

Curtail: In stair building, the outward curving portion of the hand rail and of the outer end of the lower step or steps of a flight; possibly an abbreviation of curved tail. An ample curtail to the lowest two or three steps not only enhances their appearance, but offers an easier start to persons approaching from the side. A plain semicircular curtail to the lowest step is called a bull nose.

Curtail step: The lowest step in a flight of chairs.

Curtain: (I.) (A) In fortification, the wall between two towers or bastions, and in this sense accurately descriptive of a part of the defensive works. (B) By extension, in a building having pavilions, projecting masses, and the like, the flat wall between any two such masses.

Curtain: (II.) A hanging, usually of soft and pliant material, and usually for screening, protecting, or hiding something, or for closing an opening, as a doorway. Those which hang in the church doorways of Europe are often of leather, and heavily lined and stuffed; but curtains generally are assumed to be easily movable, and even capable of being compressed into narrow folds, for which purpose they are hung on rings which slide on a rod.

Curtain wall: A portion of wall contained between two advancing structures, such as wings, pavilions, bastions, or turrets. The term indicates position, and not character or function. A curtain wall may be a mere screen, as to a court or yard, or a part of a facade; it may be solid or fenestrated, either higher or lower than its flanking structures, or of the same height. In modern construction, most often a thin subordinate wall between two piers or other supporting members; the curtain being primarily a filling and having no share-or but little-in the support of other portions of the structure. Thus, in skeleton construction, curtain walls are built between each two encased columns and usually on a girder at each floor level or thereabouts.

Curule chair: A chair with heavy curved legs and an X shaped frame.

Curve: In architectural drawing, a thin piece of wood, metal, hard rubber, or like material, cut to an outline of varied curvature for laying out, in a drawing, curves not to be produced with the ordinary forms of compasses, either because they are not arcs of circles, or because they are circular arcs of very long radius. Sets of special curves are used in ship drafting and railway plotting. One or two pieces usually suffice for the architect, each having a considerable variety of curves in its outline. Sometimes called French curve and set curve.

Cushion-back carpet: A carpet having a cushioning lining, padding or underlay material as an integral part of its backing. A designation given to a carpet with a laminated secondary backing of a resilient material such as foam rubber, or vinyl foam, sponge rubber, vinyl or similar materials.

Cushioned frieze: A convex frieze.

Custom or One-of-a-Kind Building: Any building manufactured to individual system specifications and not intended for duplication or repetitive manufacture.

Custom tufted: Carpet or rugs in which pile yarns are manually tufted with hand machines or by narrow width tufting machines.

Cut: A length of fabric, such as carpet.

Cut glass: Decorative designs carved into glass with an abrasive wheel.

Cut-off angle: (of a luminaire) The angle from the vertical at which a reflector, louver, or other shielding device cuts off direct visibility of a light source. It is the complementary angle of the shielding angle. In the case of reflector type lightshields it is also important to ascertain the cut-off angle to the reflected image of the light source as this is often almost as bright as the source itself.

Cutoff luminaries: Outdoor luminaries that restrict all light output to below 85° from vertical.

Cut Pile: A fabric, the face of which is composed of cut ends of pile yarn.

Cyma curve: A curve used for an outline of a structural element or for ornamentation in the shape of an S.

Cypress: A soft wood that smells similar to cedar.

D

"D" size sheet: 30" x 42".

Dado: (A) In Italian, a tessera or die; hence the flat face of a pedestal between the base and cap. In English it denotes a continuous pedestal or wainscot, including the base and cap molding, or sometimes only the plane surface between the base board and cap molding of such a continuous pedestal. A panelled wooden dado is generally called a wainscot; the words are often used erroneously as if synonymous. Dado is not usually used of an external pedestal course. (B) A groove formed by dadoing. (C) To cut or form with a groove or grooves of a rectangular section, as in making the upright sides of a bookcase which are so grooved to receive the ends of shelves. (D) To insert in such a groove or grooves; to perform the whole operation of connecting parts in such a manner. Thus, it may be said of a bookcase that the shelves are to be dadoed in. The term is usually applied only to such a method of connection when the groove is made to receive the full thickness of the inserted piece.

Dado, blind or stopped: A dado that is not visible when the joint is completed.

Dagger: A tracery motif in the shape of an arrow-head, pointed or rounded on the end.

Damascening: Decorative inlay of copper, silver or gold onto steel, iron or bronze.

Damask: A fabric with a flat-pattern that combines a taffeta weave against a background of satin weave. Made of cotton, linen, silk and synthetics.

Davenport: A sofa that makes into a bed; or a British writing desk.

Daybed: A bed that is also used as a sofa. It is usually set against a wall and has pillows.

Dead--(Pile yarn): The pile yarn in a Wilton carpet which remains hidden in the backing structure when not forming a pile tuft.

Decay: Disintegration of wood due to the action of wood-destroying fungi. "Doze," "rot," and "unsound wood" mean the same as decay.

Deck chair: A chair usually found on a ship with leg rests and arms made from wood and able to fold.

Decorate: To make beautiful or interesting to the eye, whether by the proper arrangement, shaping, and coloring of the essential part or by the addition of ornament, or in both ways.

Decoupage: Paper cutouts used to decorate a surface.

Deep dye: Modified synthetic fibers with increased dye affinity relative to regular dye fibers. By combining deep dye fibers with regular dye fibers, a two color effect can be achieved within one dye bath.

Deep dye printing: Deep dye printing employs a process related to screen printing. The difference lies in the use of premetalized dyes and an electrostatic charge to force the colors deep into the pile at one time.

Defect: Fault which detracts from the quality, appearance, or utility of the piece. Handling marks and/or grain raising due to moisture shall not be considered a defect.

Deflected needle: Needles in the tufting machine that are pushed aside by a warp end in the backing cloth causing a streak or "grinning" running lengthwise because of off-standard tuft spacing across the width. The real mechanism of most so-called needle deflection is the pushing aside of backing fabric warp yarns by tufting needles during tuft insertion. When the needles withdraw, warp yarns move back to their original positions, thus pushing tuft rows off gauge and creating wide gaps between them.

Delamination: The separation of layers in an assembly because of failure of the adhesive, either in the adhesive itself or at the interface between the adhesive and the lamination. For plywood, if separation between the plies is greater than 2" in continuous length, over 1/4" in depth at any part, and .003" in width, it shall be considered delamination. For solid stock, if the separation between the members is greater than 1/4" deep and more than .00" in width and the total length of all such delamination is more than 5% of the total length of the glue line, it shall be considered delaminated. If more than one delamination occurs in a single glue line, the total length of all such delamination shall determine whether or not it is considered to be delaminated.

Delftware: Earthenware of Dutch origin that has been glazed with tin.

Della Robia ware: Relief sculpture that was originated by the Della

Robbia family and that has been glazed with tin.

Demilune: (French) Semicircular. A crescent-shaped outwork built into a moat or a fort.

Den: A room for either relaxation or for family activities. It can also be called a library or a study and may be furnished according to the use of the room.

Denier: A yarn count unit. It is the weight in grams of 9,000 meters. Denier is a direct yarn numbering system; the higher the denier, the larger the yarn.

Denim: Course twilled cotton. Usually colored blue.

Density: A factor used to judge the quality of a carpet. It denotes the amount of surface yarns compressed into a given area of a carpet. The closer the pile tufts are to each other, and the more they extend above the backing, and the heavier the pile yarn, then the more punishment the carpet can take within the same fiber category. The weight of pile yarn in a unit volume of carpet. U.S. government FHA density (D), expressed in ounces per cubic yard, is given by the formula $D = T \times W$ in which D is density, W is pile yarn weight in ounces per square yard,

and T is pile thickness or height in inches.

Dent: (A) The space between wires of reed or heddles or harness through which the warp ends are drawn. (B) The space between two chains in a fabric.

Derby porcelain: China that is manufactured in Derby, England. Its earliest piece is believed to be from 1750. Derby is very ornamental using flowers and human forms as designs.

Derbyshire chair: See Yorkshire chair.

Detail drawing: A drawing showing the details of a composition, or parts of them. Such drawings are commonly made of full size, or on a scale two or three times greater than the general drawings.

Device: A pictorial or sculptured design, usually emblematic or symbolical, expressing a sentiment and often accompanied by a motto in which the same or a similar sentiment is put into words. The device (called also *impresa* or *imprezza*) was common in the sixteenth and seventeenth centuries, and a simple one or a single element or part of one is often found in architectural decoration. The device is freely taken by any person at pleasure; and it differs in this from heraldic bearings which are always the direct gift or "grant" of a superior authority.

Dhurrie: A rug that is manufactured in India and is flat and woven.

Diaper work: A repeated pattern that uses geometrical and checkered designs.

Diazo: A positive-to-positive reproduction process, rather than a positive-to-negative one like blueprinting. It is a relatively dry process. Special machines are used to expose the tracing and a sensitive paper to ultraviolet light. Then the sensitive copy is developed into a final copy. These *Diazo* copies come in blue line, brown and black line prints on bond paper, heavy presentation paper, or vellum (called Sepias). *Mylar* prints are also available. The prints are usually made on a white background. The clarity of the background depends on a high contrast between the lines drawn on the tracing and the vellum on which it is drawn. This is the reason a drafter should make clear and dark lines in the original. Very light lettering guidelines and light blue colored pencil lines are virtually invisible to the *Diazo*

machine and can be ignored when you prepare your tracing for reproduction.

Differential dyeing fibers (dye-variant fibers): Fibers, natural or man-made, so treated or modified in composition that their affinity for dyes becomes changed; i.e., to be reserved, dye lighter or dye darker than normal fibers, dependent upon the particular dyes and methods of application employed.

Dimming ballast: Special fluorescent lamp ballast, which when used with a dimmer control, permits varying light output.

Dining room: The room in which the family and guests, if any, come together and dine formally.

Direct Current (DC): Flow of electricity continuously in one direction from positive to negative.

Direct Glare: Glare resulting from high luminances or insufficiently shielded light sources in the field of view. It usually is associated with bright areas, such as luminaries, ceilings and windows which are outside the visual task or region being viewed.

Directoire style: A simple and pure style of furniture that was popular from 1795-1804. This style became more elaborate under Napoleon. Mahogany and oak were popular during this time.

Director's chair: A folding canvas covered chair.

Discharge lamp: A lamp in which light (or radiant energy near the visible spectrum) is produced by the passage of an electric current through a vapor or a gas.

Discomfort glare: Glare producing discomfort. It does not necessarily interfere with visual performance or visibility.

Distressing: See antiquing.

Distribution panel: Box containing circuit breakers or fuses where power is distributed to branch circuits.

Divan: A couch that sits against a wall and has no back or arms.

Dobby: A carpet loom device that selects the rotation in which one or more of a group of harnesses are raised over a filling shot. Can float an end over as many filling shots as desired. Produces geometric patterns in woven carpet.

Documentary: A document from the eighteenth century that has been printed on wallpaper or cloth.

Dogtooth: An ornament made of a series of four-cornered stars diagonally placed and pyramidally raised.

Dolphin: A design in the shape of a dolphin's head used on Renaissance, Louis XIV and XVI, French Empire and British Regency furniture.

Domestic: Describes carpet made in the United States.

Door: The filling, usually solid, of a doorway, so secured as to be easily opened and shut. It is much more common to support a door by hinges secured to the doorpost or frame at the side; but a door may turn on pivots at top and bottom, as frequently in antiquity, or may slide or roll up horizontally or vertically. Where the solid filling is hung by hinges at the top of the doorway, or where it slides vertically, in the manner of a portcullis, it is rarely called a door. The doors of antiquity are but little known to us; a few of bronze, belonging to the later years of the Roman Empire, still exist, and it may be said that modern doors of metal have been studied from the ancient examples. The doors of the Middle Ages were usually of solid planks set edge to edge, and secured to each other by dowels or bands, the whole being held in place by the long strip hinges having holes through which nails were driven through the wood and clinched on the other side. Panel doors are not very ancient, but their obvious superiority in lightness, in permanent retention of their plane surfaces, and in counteracting almost entirely the shrinkage of wood, has made their use almost universal. Doors have always been a favorite medium for ornamentation.

Door hanger: A hanger for the support of a sliding door, especially such a door when hung from above. The meaning of the term is usually extended to mean the entire apparatus for such purpose, including the track or rails from which the door may be supported.

Doorstep: (A) The sill of a doorway; that upon which one steps in passing from a lower level through the doorway. (B) By extension, the platform with two or three steps outside of an outer door.

Doorway: An opening for entrance to, and exit from, a building or part of a building; such an opening, together with its immediate surroundings.

Door, window, and room finish schedules: Charts of blueprints that give information about doors, windows, etc.

Dope dyed: (See also Solution dyed and Spun dyed) Synthetic fibers colored by addition of pigments to polymer melts or solutions prior to extrusion by the fiber producer.

Dos-a-dos: (French) Chair with two attached seats which face in opposite directions.

Double back: (See also Secondary Backing) Woven or nonwoven fabric laminated to the back of carpet with latex or other adhesive. Double-backed carpets have enhanced dimensional stability and strength.

Double faced molding: A metal strip designed to protect the abutting edges of two fabrics with different degrees of dimensional stability against raveling and wear.

Double Hung: (A) Furnished with, or made up of, two sashes one above the other, arranged to slide vertically past each other; said of a window. Old houses, both in America and in England, often have only one of the two sashes hung with weights; the other being fixed, or, if movable, held in place by means of a button or prop; such may be said to be single hung. (B) Hung on both sides with cord and pulley; said only of vertical sliding sash. In some cases, where windows are narrow, or are divided by mullions into narrow lights, a window box with cord, pulley, and weight is furnished on one side only, the other side of the sash being sometimes fitted with rollers to facilitate its movement. Such sash may be said to be single hung.

Dovetail, blind: A dovetail joint that is not visible when the joint is completed.

Dovetail, lap: A dovetail for joining two boards, as at a corner, in which part of the thickness of one board overlaps the end of the other. Thus, the dovetail of the overlapping board is formed, as it were, in the angle of a rebate which receives the end of the other board. It is frequently formed as a Secret Dovetail.

Dowel: (A) A pin, or similar projecting member, to connect two parts together. It may be formed on one of the two parts to be united and fitted to an aperture in the other; or, more commonly, a separate member, as a short rod, or the like, inserted part way into each piece. (B) Wood peg or metal screw used to

strengthen a wood joint. Also see cramp.

Doweled: A joint using dowels (doweled construction); also doweled edge joint.

Dower furniture: A chest that is considered a bridal or dowry chest, originally used to hold linens and other items belonging to the prospective bride.

Downlight: Surface mounted or suspended direct lighting.

Drafting brush: A tool for dusting erasure leavings and graphite dust off tracings and drawing board.

Drafting tape: Tape similar to masking tape but not as sticky. It is used to hold tracing paper to the drafting board without damaging the paper or the drawing surface. Drafting tape is also less likely to leave gum on the paper and drafting board. 3/4" wide tape is the best all-around size.

Draftsman: One more or less skilled in drafting; specifically, one whose business it is to draw and prepare plans and designs, as for an architect. Also written Draughtsman.

Draperies: Coverings made to open or close across windows and control sunlight.

Draw: The manner and rotation in which the warp ends are placed in the loom heddles and reeds.

Drawing inks: Inks that have a reasonable degree of permanence if kept from sunlight or strong diffused light. Shellac is the usual waterproofing ingredient, therefore it is necessary to thoroughly clean pens, instruments and brushes after use. To dilute black ink, add pure water with four drops of aqua ammonia to the ounce. Tap water will suffice for washes which are applied at once. To dilute colored inks, use pure water only. Never add any acid or mix ink brands.

Drawing-In or Drawing-Up: The process of placing the warp ends through the heddles and reeds of the loom.

Draw table: See refectory table.

Dresden: See Meissen.

Dresser: (A) A chest of drawers usually 36" high; also can refer to a Gothic sideboard used to prepare food. (B) A table, shelf, or set of shelves upon which vessels for use at meals are kept permanently.

Originally, the dresser served as a carving table and place of preparation for the dishes about to be served; that is to say, it was there that the dressings of the table were prepared.

Dressing table: A table with a mirror that allows one to sit in front and apply make-up.

Drill: A punch or boring instrument operated mechanically to drive holes through any hard material, as rock or metal, either by being rapidly rotated or by being caused to give blows.

Drop-in seat: See slip seat.

Drop-leaf table: A table that has extentions at each end and lengthens the table when they are raised.

Drop match: A design in a carpet surface that drops every other repeat down part of its length to produce a diagonal alignment of the designs across the width of the carpet. A pattern in printed, high-low, cutloop, or figured woven carpet which repeats diagonally. Each corresponding pattern element drops down a certain distance, usually a half pattern repeat in length, instead of simply repeating horizontally across the width as in set match.

Drop ornament: A carved ornament in the form of a pendent.

Drop shipment: Any shipment which does not go directly to the interior designer but to the client or another address.

Drum table: A table made in the shape of a drum.

Dry cleaning powder: A dust sprinkled on the tracing as the drafter works. It keeps the tracing clean of graphite smudges. It is best not to rub it on the paper. The material is similar to eraser dust, and absorbs the loose graphite dust that can smudge drafting paper.

Dry foam: A detergent solution containing only a small amount of water is mechanically worked into the surface of the carpet and the loose soil is removed by a vacuum.

Dry point: An engraving technique used on a copper tale without using acid.

Dry Rot: (A) A condition caused by attack by microorganisms on fibers, textiles, carpets or other materials, characterized by loss of strength and integrity. Attack on carpet backings permits carpet to break and tear easily. Cellulosics such as jute are susceptible whereas polypropylene

and most other synthetics are virtually immune. (B) Decay in wood of which the primary cause is dampness, and, especially, lack of ventilation. If the end of a timber is built up too closely in a wall, or enclosed in an iron shoe, it will be attacked by this decay, even if well seasoned.

Dry sink: A sink used as a planter or a bar.

Dry-wet vacuum: A vacuum cleaner with the built-in capability to pick up liquids as well as dry material.

Duchesse-brisee: (French) Chaise-longue with a separate footpiece.

Duchesse: (French) A nineteenth century chaise longue with two bergeres and an ottoman.

Duck: See canvas.

Duck foot: See pad foot.

Dust board: A board placed between drawers of a chest to protect against dust.

Dust ruffle: Skirting that hangs from the box spring of a bed to the floor.

Dutch colonial style: Furniture style characterized by over hanging eaves and gambrel roofs. It was popular in the seventeenth century in the Dutch-settled sections of the North American colonies.

Dutch cupboard: A buffet with shelves used to display china.

Dutch door: A door split down the middle allowing each half to open separately.

Dutchman: A piece of wood or other material used to cover an opening or defect on another piece of wood or material.

Dutchman: Installer's term for a narrow strip seamed onto standard width carpet to fit oddly dimensioned areas. Proper planning will minimize the need for this practice.

Dutch settle: An eighteenth to nineteenth century piece of furniture that has a back hinged so that it can be lowered into a table.

Dye beck: A large vat for piece dyeing carpet by immersion in aqueous solutions of dyes and chemicals. Fitted with a reel for circulating carpet in and out of the dye liquor, inlets for steam and water, drains, and temperature controls.

Dyeing: Coloring fibers, yarns, fabrics, carpets or other materials by addition or incorporation of small amounts (usually 1% or less) of highly colored materials known as dyes and pigments.

Dyestuff (or Dye): A highly colored substance capable of permanent physical or chemical attachment to textile fibers; coloration of fibers occurs upon attachment of small quantities. Most dyes are applied from water solutions or dispersions.

E

Eagle: The official seal of the United States of America adopted by Congress in 1786.

Ears: Wings of a wing chair.

Earthenware: All pottery that has been hardened by fire and made from clay.

Eased edge: Slightly rounded edge not to exceed 1/16" radius, to remove sharp corners.

Easy chair: Any comfortable chair.

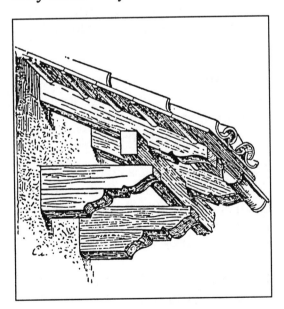

Eaves: The lower portion of a sloping projection beyond the walls, and forming an overhanging drip for water.

Ebony: A hard wood, black in color and used for furniture and piano keys. It is a tropical wood and polishes well.

Eclecticism: Combining several styles to achieve a desired effect.

Ecran: (French) Screen.

Ecran-a-cheval: (French) A sliding panel frame used as a fire screen.

Edge band, concealed: Not more than 1/16" of the edge band shall show on the face of the plywood or particleboard.

Edge finish molding: A rigid or flexible material that protects the cut edge of a carpet against unraveling or wear.

Edging: The operation of trimming the edges, that is, the narrow, upper or lower faces of rafters, joists, or ribs to a required plane or surface, whether by cutting down or furring out; called also Ranging (cf. Backing).

Efficacy: See Lamp Efficacy.

Egg and anchor; egg and dart: A decoration border of ovals and darts or anchors in a running pattern. It was common in classical architecture.

Egg and tongue: An ornament applied to a convex rounded molding, and consisting of a series of approximately oval projecting rounded surfaces of small size, each one surrounded by a groove and a raised rim, between which rims are inserted, one between every pair of the "eggs" with their enclosing ridges, a sharp-pointed member calculated to contrast in the most forcible way with the soft rounded surfaces between which it is set. This pointed member is called dart, or anchor, or tongue, according to its shape, and the name of the ornament is sometimes varied accordingly. Ornaments of this kind are found in Greek buildings of the Ionic style, dating from a time as early as the fourth century B.C. It is there varied from the plainest nearly egg-shaped rounds with mere ridges following their contour, and others as simply taking the place of the darts between, to a much more elaborate design in which the eggs are turned into leaves with midribs strongly marked, and the darts between modified in a like direction. They are also even in the placing, from the chief ornament of the cap molding and several inches in height, to one of many horizontal parallel bands, each as small as allows of effective working of the ornament in marble. The ornament was taken as the single decoration of the Roman Doric capital; the ovolo so decorated is the chief characteristic of this order.

Eggshell china or porcelain: A very thin porcelain that originated in fifteenth century China.

Egyptian style: A style characterized by pyramids, lotus columns and pylons originated by the ancient Egyptians.

Electric eraser: A basic tool of the drafter, and comes in both cord and cordless types. It saves time and makes a much neater tracing than conventional erasers.

Electrical closet: A small room that holds electrical equipment.

Electrical seaming: A seaming method that uses an electric current to activate a thermoplastic adhesive coated on a specialized seaming tape.

Electrostatic flocking: A method used for producing flocked fabrics, including flocked carpet. Flocking consists of attaching short lengths of fibers to fabric substratums with adhesives. In electrostatic flocking, precision cut fibers are aligned in an electrostatic field perpendicular to the substratum, thus creating a plush-like surface.

Elevation: A drawing which represents a vertical right line projection of anything, especially the exterior of a building or part of a building on one side, or any part thereof.

Elizabethan style: A style of furniture with Renaissance carvings, baluster turnings and gadroons. It was developed from 1558-1603 and isn't often seen in America today.

Elliptical Reflector: (ER) Lamp whose reflector focuses the light about 2" ahead of the bulb, reducing light loss when used in deep baffle downlights.

Elm: A hard wood light brown in color and used chiefly for veneering and flooring.

Embossed: A wallcovering with a three-dimensional design impressed in the surface by pressure and/or heat.

Embossed pattern: The type of pattern formed in a carpet when heavy twisted pile tufts are used in a ground of straight pile tufts to form an engraved effect.

Embossed work: In general, decorative work in relief, produced not by carving or casting, but by stamping, hammering, pressing with a die, or like use of mechanical force; such as that done in sheet metal by "striking up" from behind.

Embossing: A design impressed into the back of metal, leather or fabric with hot rollers.

Embroidery: A type of decorated needlework.

Empire style: A neoclassic style that originated from the French First Empire and was very elaborate.

Enamel: A variety of glass which is used especially for decorative work; either inlaid in another surface, as of metal, or forming a mosaic with a metal ground or frame to hold it in place, or covering the whole surface. By means of enamel, decoration of church vessels and pieces of domestic use and adornment is made easy and effective. The term enamelling, applied to the process of laying enamel upon a surface or of adorning an object with enamel, is extended to mean, in the popular sense, a certain kind of finish by means of paint and varnish.

Encaustic: Fixed by heat; applied by any process to which heat is essential.

Encaustic painting: Literally, a painting which implies the application of heat either during or subsequent to its execution. This process is said to have been much employed by the Greeks both for mural and easel pictures, as well as for ships; nor was its use confined to the Greeks. As a mural process it was ultimately replaced by fresco. Encaustic implies a burning, The colors being mixed with wax. Unfortunately the words encaustic and wax were often used by ancient authors synonymously for painting and color, hence great confusion and uncertainty. No specimen of an important encaustic mural painting by Greek artists has been preserved. Greco-Egyptian mummy masks of a late period have been recently discovered, and it is asserted that some of these were painted by the encaustic process; others in tempera; others, again, in both tempera and encaustic. The celebrated head called *The Muse of Cortona*, preserved in the museum of that town, is said to have been painted in wax. Vitruvious gives as a receipt for the preservation of vermillion-colored walls exposed to the sun, a final coat of Punic wax and oil cauterized, and subsequently rubbed with a candle and fine linen. The mural paintings of Pompeii, Rome, and its environs were probably painted in fresco, sometimes in tempera, or in a combination of the two methods. Colors are melted with wax and resin, then applied with a brush, and afterward modelled with heated instruments called cauteria. Any wax painting when completed may, or may not, be burnt in by the application of heat. The effect of the burning is to give a slight glass to the surface, increase the depth of the tone, blend the modelling, and cause the colors to penetrate more deeply the wall surface, if the latter be absorbent. The Greeks knew of the dissolution of wax by a volatile or essential oil, such as turpentine.

Encoignure: (French) A desk that contains hidden drawers and many compartments. A corner cabinet or table.

Encrier: (French) Inkwell.

End: (A) An individual warp yarn in woven fabric. (B) An individual pile yarn in tufted carpet. (C) A roll end, or short length of carpet; or a remnant.

End table: A small table used beside a chair or sofa.

Enfilade: Alignment of interior doors so that a view is created through the series of open doors. Indicative of French Baroque palace design.

Engraving: The art and practice of making incisions in a hard material with a sharp tool. By extension, the producing of a similar effect by a mordant liquid (as in etching); but the term is restricted to such sinkings as are produced by the taking away of a solid material, being distinguished in this from chasing. In architectural practice, engraving has to do with memorial brasses and bronze plates, such as are let into the pedestals of statues or, if decorative, on the walls of buildings, where they are used especially for record; and equally for incised work in stone, which, however, when limited to lettering, is more often called inscription.

Entresol: (French) A mezzanine floor.

Entry: Originally, that part of a building by which access was had to its interior. Used indifferently for the doorway itself, the passage to which it leads, the outer porch, or all together; as in Macbeth, II.,1: "I hear a knocking . . at the south entry." Later: (A) In England, an alley or unimportant street leading to another street or public place. (B) In the United States, a passage in a house; more usually the principal passage leading from the front door, but frequently any passage, and even a staircase hall.

Epergne: A centerpiece used to hold flowers, candy or nuts made of glass or silver.

Epoxy: A plastic that is flexible and resistant to corrosion and weather. It is used for surface protective coverings, bonding agent for metal, wood, ceramics and rubber.

Equipment: All equipment, materials, appliances, devices, fixtures, fittings or accessories installed in or used in a building.

Equivalent Sphere Illumination: (ESI) The level of sphere illumination which would produce task visibility equivalent to that produced by a specific lighting environment. Suppose a task at a given location and direction of view within a specific lighting system has 100 fc of illumination. Suppose this same task is now viewed under sphere lighting and the sphere lighting level is adjusted so that the task visibility is the same under the sphere lighting as it was under the lighting system. Suppose the lighting level at the task from the sphere lighting is 50 fc for equal visibility. Then the Equivalent Sphere Illumination of the task under the lighting system would be 50 ESI fc.

Eraser shield: A stainless steel template with multiple shaped holes used to expose only those parts of a drawing to be erased and masking off the rest. It is laid over the pencil mark with the error exposed through an opening in order to erase. The steel part protects the good line and makes a much neater correction.

Escabelle: (French) A trestle chair.

Escritoire: A desk that contains hidden drawers and many compartments.

Escutcheon: (A) In heraldry, the surface upon which are charged the devices born by any one as peculiar and distinctive to him or her. The form of the escutcheon is generally shield-like, affecting the outline of the knight's shield as employed at any epoch; but, in the neoclassic art of the seventeenth and eighteenth centuries, it is often an oval and sometimes surrounded by scrollwork, while the escutcheon born by women is lozenge-shaped. The charges should be applied to the escutcheon in color, but it has been recognized at all epochs that a slight relief may be made to answer the purpose; thus, a fesse or pale charged upon an escutcheon may be represented in sculpture by very slight relief from the surface or field of the escutcheon,-a relief only sufficient to cast a slight shadow at its edge. (B) By extension, from the above definition, a small plate or the like, generally of metal and more or less ornamental, used for many specific purposes; as about a keyhole to protect the edges and pierced to admit the key; or inscribed with a name or number as a doorplate. (C) A metal plate used to protect veneering around a keyhole.

Espangnolette: A sculpture of a female bust in bronze or wood.

Etagere: (French)A cabinet with shelves that display accessories.

Etui: (French) Container or box.

Eventail: (French) Fan.

Ewer: A pitcher that holds water used to wash hands after eating.

Exception: A term indicating an acceptable alternative to a standard or code.

Exit: A gateway or doorway intended to serve only for persons leaving a building or enclosure, especially when prepared for use when a great crowd is dispersing. In some public buildings, such as theaters, there are exits for ordinary communications and others especially prepared for use in case of alarm.

Exposed surfaces: Surfaces visible after installation, except for exposed portions of casework.

Extended length: The length of pile yarn in one running inch of one tuft row in tufted carpet. Sometimes called take-up.

Extended life lamps: Incandescent lamps that have an average rated life of 2,500 or more hours and reduced light output compared to standard general service lamps of the same wattage.

F

Fabric classification: In flammability testing classifications are based either on the ability of a fabric or fabrics to withstand ignition from a nonflaming source or an open flame or on specific construction, finish application, fiber content, and nominal weight per unit area.

Fabricating: Thermoplastics and thermosettings are turned into tubes, sheets, rods, and films. There are three categories of fabricating. (A) Machining, in which materials are ground, reamed, milled, and drilled. This process is done to tubes, rods, and rigid sheets. (B) Cutting-Sewing-Sealing of film and Sheets, in which films and sheets are cut into patterns and made into raincoats, luggage, and toys. (C) Forming, in which thermoplastic sheets are cut into the approximate shape and folded into final form. The sheets are turned into shapes by a vacuum or by molding.

Fabric-backed: A wallcovering with a backing of woven or knitted yarns or a nonwoven structure of randomly distributed textile fibers.

Fabric classification: In flammability testing, classifications are based either on the ability of a fabric or fabrics to withstand ignition from a nonflaming source or an open flame or on specific construction, finish application, fiber content, and nominal weight per unit area.

Facade: The architectural front of a building; not necessarily the principal front, but any face or presentation of a structure which is nearly in one plane, and is treated in the main as a single vertical wall with but minor modifications. Thus, if a large building presents toward one street a front consisting of the ends of two projecting wings with a low wall between them enclosing a courtyard, that would be hardly a facade, but rather two facades of the two pavilions. With buildings which present on all sides fronts of similar or equivalent elaborateness of treatment, it is, perhaps, incorrect to speak of a facade; thus, in a great church, although the west front may be described by this term, it is inaccurate because that front would not be what it is were it presented without the flanks or north and south sides. The facade rather comes of street architecture and of buildings which have but one front considered of sufficient importance to receive architectural treatment.

Face seams: Sewed or cemented seams made without turning the carpet over or face-down. They are used during installations when back seaming is impossible.

Fadeometer: Device for determining the effects of light on the properties of yarns, fibers, fabrics, carpets, plastic, and other materials. It uses a standard light source such as a xenon arc lamp to simulate approximately the spectrum of sunlight. Generally used for measuring fade resistance of carpet colors which are rated according to the number of hours of fadeometer exposure required to produce visible loss of color.

Fading: Loss of color. Caused by actinic radiation such as sunlight or artificial light, atmospheric gases including ozone, nitric oxide, and hydrogen sulfide, cleaning and bleaching chemicals such as sodium hypochlorite, and other household and industrial products, chlorine chemicals or swimming pools, and other factors. Commercial installations in areas where such exposures occur require extreme care in selection of colorfast carpet.

Faience: (French) Terra cotta. Pottery of coarse or dark colored body covered by an opaque coating, such as enamel, which may be elaborated painted. This is the proper signification, and it covers all the beautiful decorative wares of Italy from the fifteenth to the eighteenth centuries, including the richest varieties of majolica, and also the various potteries of France of slightly later epochs, such as those of Rouen, Nevers, Moustiers, and many more. These wares are often very soft, both enamel and body; but when used for external decoration such as wall tiles and the like, the same effects of color and brilliancy are possible with an extremely hard and enduring substance, and the greatest epoch have been marked by the production of cresting tiles, ridge tiles, finials for painted roofs, and the like, which are perfectly durable.

Family room: See den.

Fan-back chair: A chair that has vertical spindles that fan out from the seat to the top rail.

Fanlight: A semi-circular window over a door. Common in Georgian and Regency architecture.

Fascia: A nailed board, under the eaves of a building, used for facing. A plain horizontal band in an architrave.

Fastness: Retention of color by carpets or other materials, usually with reference to specific exposures, e.g., lightfastness and washfastness. Dyestuff, fiber type, and dyeing method all influence the ability of colored carpets and fabrics to withstand the effects of color destroying agents.

Fauteuil: (French) An upholstered armchair with open arms.

Faux: A French term for something that is an imitation such as simulated wood or marble.

Fees and compensations: Prices set by the interior designer for work completed. Designers charge on a per hour basis, a flat rate and a percentage mark-up.

Felt: Unwoven fabric made by matting and compressing fibers, usually wool, with heat and moisture.

Felting: A nonwoven fabric formation process comprising entanglement of fibers by mechanical or other means. The product is called felt. Felts made by needle entanglement of solution dyed fibers such as polypropylene are used as outdoor carpet. Unlike weaving and tufting, felting does not employ yarns but converts fiber directly to fabric.

Fender: A metal guard used by a fireplace to protect against sparks or logs.

Fenestration: The arrangement of windows in a building.

Festoon: A carved ornament in the shape of a garland of fruit and flowers. Cloth that hangs over a poster bed, or carvings in the shape of leaves, foliage or fruit.

Fiber cushion: Separate carpet underpad consisting of needle-felted animal hair, jute, other fibers, or fiber blends. Hair and jute blends are common. Some padding felts are rubberized and may have one or two rubber faces.

Fiberglass: Fabric made from glass fibers.

Fibers: Natural or man-made objects having very high aspect ratios, that is, having lengths hundreds to thousands of times greater than their widths. Useful textile fibers have high tensile strengths, flexibility, and resistance to heat, light, chemicals, and abrasives.

Fiddle back: An eighteenth century chair with one splat that looks similar to a violin.

Fielded panel: A panel with a plain raised central area.

Filament: A single continuous strand of natural or synthetic fiber.

Filigree: Gold and silver intertwined into a pattern similar to lace often used on jewelry and furniture.

Filler: A low cost material used for extending rubber, plastic, or other polymers. Fillers are generally powders of very small particle size. Carpet latex laminating compounds and foams contain large amounts of fillers. The most common filler in carpet latex is finely powdered calcium carbonate, often called whiting, produced by grinding limestone.

Filling yarn: In weaving, any yarn running across the width of the fabric perpendicular to the warp yarns. In woven carpet, filling yarns are part of the group of construction yarns which also include chain and stuffer warp and form the backing. Woven carpet fill and chain warp yarns interface to secure the pile yarns. Filling and other construction yarns usually are fibrillated polypropylene, jute, kraftcord, or similar materials.

Film yarn: Yarn produced by slitting extruded films into narrow strips. Slit film polypropylene yarns are woven into fabrics used as primary backings in tufted carpets.

Finger: A series of fingers machined on the ends of two pieces of wood to be joined, which mesh together and are securely glued in position.

Finial: A knob in the shape of fruit of foliage used as decoration found on the top of a bedpost of a lamp. The terminating ornament of a gable, canopy, rod or post.

Finish: (A) Elegance or refinement in a completed piece of work; especially in the workmanship or mechanical excellence of the work as distinguished from its design or significance. It is to be observed, however, that in some kinds of work the significance itself depends upon high or elaborate finish. Thus, in Florentine mosaic as applied to walls, or marble inlay as applied to pavements, the intended effect is not obtained without very perfect workmanship. (B) Those parts of the fittings of a building which come after the heavy work of masonry, flooring, etc., has been done, and which are generally in plain sight and are closely connected with the final appearance of the building. The term is especially applied to interior work and often in connection with some other word forming a compound term.

Finished seam: A completed seam finished by bringing any trapped tufts of pile to the surface and trimming any protruding tufts level with the surrounding tufts.

Finishing: A collective term denoting processing of carpets and textiles subsequent to tufting, weaving, and dyeing. Carpet finishing processes include shearing, brushing, application of secondary backing, application of attached foam cushion, application of soil retardant and antistatic chemicals, back beating, steaming, and others.

Fir: A soft yet durable wood of evergreen trees used for interior parts of furniture.

Fire screen: A screen in front of a fireplace to prevent flying sparks of embers.

Flame: In regard to textile flammability, a flame is a hot luminous zone of gas or matter in gaseous suspension, or both, that is undergoing combustion, that is relatively constant in size and shape, and that produces a relatively low heat flux.

Flash coving: The covering of the baseboard with carpet either by separate pieces or extending the wall to wall carpet up the baseboard.

Flashing: Pieces of sheet metal covering the joints or angles between a roof and any vertical surface against which it abuts, as of a wall, parapet, or chimney, to prevent the leakage or driving in of rain water; also, such pieces covering the hips and valleys of shingle or slate roofs, or the like; or covering the joints about window frames, etc., in frame buildings. Plain flashing is formed with a single strip turned up a few inches against the vertical surface to which it is tacked or otherwise secured, and running up under the slates, tiles, or shingles to a slightly higher level. For greater security an apron, usually of lead, may be affixed to the wall above the first strip, which it overlaps; the apron being driven into the joints of the masonry protects the joint of the flashing proper. Against a brick chimney or gable parapet the sloping joint is protected by step flashing; short pieces overlapping like slates replace the continuous strip, each turned into a different horizontal joint of the brickwork. Flashings against stonework are driven into grooves cut to receive them. In all cases the joint is cemented with common or elastic cement.

Flat: A finish without gloss or luster.

Flatware: Flat dishes and spoons, forks and knives.

Flax: Vegetable fiber used to make linen. Strong but tends to wrinkle.

Flemish scroll: Two scrolls curved in the shape of a C found on chair legs.

Fleur-de-lis: (French) A lily flower. The French royal lily used as decoration on furniture.

Fleuron: A carved flower or leaf.

Flexible curve: A drawing device that can take the place of French Curves, and at the same time allows creation of customized shapes. It also allows drafters to transfer a shape from one drawing to another.

Flight: An unbroken run of stairs.

Flint glass: A very lustrous lead oxide glass developed in 1674 by George Ravenscroft.

Flip-top table: A table that folds out to increase the size of a table.

Flitch: (A) A plank, or similar thin piece, secured to the side of a beam with which it corresponds in length and depth, or nearly so, and which it serves to strengthen; one of several such pieces or beams secured together side by side to form a larger beam or girder. (B) Same as slab.

(C) A lengthwise cut in a tree from its trunk.

Flocked carpets: This construction is made by means of a unique electrostatic process. First, an especially formulated finish is applied to very short strands of pile fibers, usually of nylon. Then a pre-fabricated backing sheet, usually of jute, is coated with a heavy layer of adhesive. Next, the pretreated fibers are given an electrostatic charge which hurls the strands into the coated backing where the fibers become imbedded in the adhesive in an upright position. As many as 18,000 pile fibers per square inch are fastened to the backing in this manner. Then a suitable secondary back is laminated to the fabric and the adhesive is cured. The pile fibers are dyed either before the flocking process begins or a printing process is used on the finished carpet.

Flocking: Short, chopped fiber or flock is adhered, usually by electrostatic processes, to a base fabric, resulting in a short pile material with a velvety texture.

Floodlighting: A system designed for lighting a scene or object to a luminance greater than its surroundings. It may be for utility, advertising or decorative purposes.

Flooring: Materials used to lay a floor.

Floor plan: A sketch showing the doors, windows and interior design.

Flounce: A piece of fabric used to conceal the bottom of a chair.

Fluffing: Appearance on carpet surface of loose fiber fragments left during manufacture; not a defect but a characteristic which disappears after carpet use and vacuuming. Sometimes called fuzzing or shedding.

Fluorescent lamp: A low-pressure mercury electric-discharge lamp in which a fluorescing coating (phosphor) transforms some of the ultraviolet energy generated by the discharge into light.

Flush: Even with, in the same plane with, something else, whether adjacent or not; in exact alignment with the surrounding surface. Thus, a flush panel has its surface in the same plane with the surrounding frame; two piers having the same projection from a wall may be said to have their outer faces flush. Within 1/4". maximum protrusion from surrounding surfaces.

Flush door: A door that is level with framework and flush.

Flux: Continuous flow of luminous energy.

F.O.B.: Free On Board. Point from which a purchaser pays freight when purchasing a product.

Focal point: The point of a room that is emphasized such as, a fireplace or a view.

Foliated: An object carved with leaf ornament.

Footcandle: (fc) The unit of illuminance when the foot is taken as the unit of length. It is the illuminance on a surface one square foot in area on which there is a uniformly distributed flux of one lumen.

Foot Lambert: (fl) A unit of luminance of a perfectly diffusing surface emitting or reflecting light at the rate of one lumen per square foot.

Formica: See laminate.

Fortuny print: Hand-blocked cotton print. Made in Italy.

Four-poster bed: An eighteenth century bed having four posts one on each corner of the bed.

Foyer: The entrance hall or entrance vestibule of a building.

Franklin stove: A stove invented by Benjamin Franklin similar to a fireplace but more heat efficient.

Free Form: A floor area bounded by walls and of nonrectangular shape. Sometimes called "form-fit area." Describes either a non-rectangular shaped floor area, or an irregular shaped finishing edge of carpet, or a flexible metal or vinyl molding used to protect an irregular shaped edge of carpet from unraveling and wear.

French curves: Plastic drafting tools used to draw curved segments of objects or plans. They are drawn against with pencil or pen after an appropriate segment is selected. A selection of two or three is usually enough for architectural drafting.

French doors: Two doors that are joined together and open in the middle and have glass panes.

French polish: A furniture polish containing alcohol or oil and when applied several times achieves a high gloss finish.

French provincial style: A country style of furniture modeled after Paris fashions.

French window: A window similar to a french door.

Fresco: A painting painted on wet lime plaster.

Fret: (A) Same as meander. (B) A similar ornamentation by means of right lines forming angles with one another but carried over a larger surface. Thus, certain Oriental gratings or screens made ornamental by slender lines of wood or metal breaking one another at angles are, in the sense of their decorative design, frets, but hardly meanders. (C) Geometrical ornamental band made up of vertical and horizontal straight lines

Fretwork: An eighteenth century Chinese motif carved in low relief.

Frieze: (A) (Pronounced "freeze") A tightly twisted yarn that gives a rough, nubby appearance to carpet pile, and carpet having this characteristic. (B) A decorated strip along the upper section of a wall. The middle division of an entablature.

Fringe: Trimmed thread or cord hanging at the top in a decorative fashion.

Fruitwood: Wood from any fruit tree used in making cabinets.

Fulham stoneware: Earthenware that is transparent and regarded as the link to porcelain.

Full roll: A length of carpet or roll goods usually approximately 100 feet long. Also called a shipping roll by carpet manufacturers'. Shipping roll standards vary and may be as short as 30 feet depending upon carpet thickness and manufacturers' quality criteria. In the United States almost all roll goods are twelve or fifteen feet wide, with twelve-foot predominant.

Fumed oak: Oak wood that has been exposed to ammonia fumes giving it an antique appearance.

Fungicide: A substance which retards or prevents fungi growth.

Fur: To apply Furring. A ceiling which is suspended some distance below the joists, by means of furring, is said to be furred *down*; a roof which is carried on furring some distance above the roof beams is said to be furred *up*; a wall which is furred is said to be furred *out*.

Furniture arrangement: An arrangement of furniture conducive to the style of the occupant.

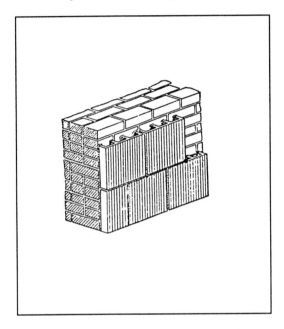

Furring: A light framework, or simply strips, generally of wood, but sometimes of metal, applied to walls, beams, or similar surfaces to support sheathing, plaster, or other form of finish. Its purpose is either to give a more uniform and even structure for the application of such a finish; or to form an air space behind such a finish; or to give a semblance of a constructive form, as the imitation of a vault, by means of some plastic material carried on a frame of the necessary shape. By extension, in recent times, hollow brick or tile used for such purposes.

Fuse: Replaceable safety device to prevent excess current flow. \

Furring strip: Any strip, generally of wood, used for furring. Specifically, in the United States, a strip of spruce, 1 inch by 2 inches in size, used chiefly in furring on the inner face of an outside wall to form an air space.

Fusion bonded carpet: The pile tufts of this type of carpet construction are first inserted into a liquid vinyl compound. These components are then fuse bonded together to produce a carpet with a continuous impermeable vinyl back and an exceptionally strong tuft retention. It is usually fabricated with a cut pile.

Fuzzing: Hairy effect on fabric surface caused by wild fibers or slack yarn twist, by fibers slipping out of yarn in either service or wet cleaning. It is corrected by shearing in manufacturing and by the professional cleaner. Carpet of continuous filament yarn is fuzzed by filament snagging and breaking.

G

Gadroon: Ridges and flutings carved into the rim of furniture.

Gadrooned: Decorated with convex curves.

Galloon: Trim used on upholstered furniture that looks like a braid.

Galvanized iron: Iron coated with zinc. The purpose of so protecting iron is to prevent rusting by keeping the moisture from its surface. It is, however, common to paint thoroughly all articles of galvanized iron as soon as they are put into place. (A) Properly, iron which has been covered first with tin by galvanic action, and subsequently with zinc by immersion in a bath. (B) In common usage, but improperly, iron which has been so coated by a non-galvanic process; having been immersed hot in a bath of zinc and other chemicals which form an alloy on the surface of the iron.

Game table: A seventeenth century table that is used to play board games. It originally had needlepoint on the top but by the eighteenth century the top was designed for chess or backgammon.

Garden stool: A seat made of wood, stone or porcelain in a barrel shape.

Garde-robe: (French) Wardrobe.

Garderobe: A wardrobe.

Gargoyle: A carved grotesque figure which extends from a roof and serves as a water spout.

Garniture: (French) Any decoration or motif.

Gate-leg table: A sixteenth century table with legs that close like a gate and leaves that hang down and are supported by the legs.

Gauge: (A) To bring to a given size or a given dimension, as thickness, or the like. The term properly signifies to test or measure, but it is in common use as implying the rubbing, cutting, or other process which brings the object into shape. Thus, the bricks required for the voussoirs of an arch which is to be ornamental in character, especially if small in proportion to the size of the material, are commonly specified to be gauged and rubbed; that is, brought to the exact size and shape and rubbed smooth. (B) In plastering, to prepare or mix with plaster of Paris; the term meaning originally to measure the quantities, then to mix such measured quantities, finally, to mix especially those ingredients which are submitted to careful measurement. (C) In roofing, the exposed portion of a slate, tile, or the like, when laid in place. (D) The closeness of the pile rows in tufted or knitted fabrics as measured across the width of the carpet. For example 1/8 of an inch means the pile rows are 1/8 of an inch apart the entire width of the carpet. The higher the number the closer the pile tufts are to each other widthwise.

Gauge/Pitch: The number of ends of surface yarn counting across the width of carpet. In woven carpet, pitch is the number of ends of yarn in 27 inches of width; e.g., 216 divided by 27 = 8 ends per inch. In tufted carpet, gauge also means the number of ends of surface yarn per inch counting across the carpet; e.g., 1/8 gauge = 8 ends per inch. To convert gauge to pitch, multiply ends per inch by 27; e.g., 1/10 gauge is equivalent to 270 pitch, or 10 ends per inch x 27. One-eighth gauge is 8 ends of yarn per inch x 27 = 216 pitch.

Gauge wire: A standing wire used with an extra filling yarn to control the height of the pile on a carpet weaving loom.

General lighting: See Ambient Lighting.

General service lamps: A or PS incandescent lamps.

Geometrical decorated: In English architecture, belonging to the Decorated style characteristic of the thirteenth century, and having much geometrical tracery. The term is one of many attempts at a minute and classified nomenclature which it is probably impossible to secure.

German silver: An alloy, known as nickel silver, composed of copper, tin, and nickel. It is corrosion resistant and malleable.

Gesso: A mix applied as a base coat for decorative painting consisting of glue and linseed oil.

Gilding: (A) The art or practice of applying gold leaf or gold powder to the surface of anything, so as to give it, the appearance of gold. In thin layers of gold leaf used as a finish on wood or metal. (B) The surface and metallic appearance given by any of the processes referred to under A, as in the phrase, there is too much gilding in the decoration. Much the best and most permanent method of gilding is to apply a very thin layer of pure gold, usually called gold leaf. It is, however, easy to give to a molding or raised ornament the appearance of being solidly gilded without much use of the leaf; for the production of this effect a peculiar shade of yellowish color is employed under the general name gold color, and only those parts receive the actual metal which will received and reflect the light the most strongly. The greatest artists in the use of pure and strong color use gold with much freedom. Thus, in some of the finest Chinese enamels, it is evident that the gold line separating the small patches of color is relied upon for a background or relief to keep the whole in place. In gilding for decorative effect it is not the metal which is very costly; it is the necessity of going over the work at least twice, first with gold size, and afterward with the gold leaf, which has to be very carefully handled, applied, allowed to dry, and then rubbed, that the loose fragments may be removed.

Gimp: Braided trim used on upholstered furniture to hide tacks and for decoration.

Ginger jar: A jar used to preserve ginger, globular in shape, made of Chinese ceramic.

Gingham: Plain-weave, yarn-dyed cotton fabric with a checkered or striped pattern.

Girandole: A wall bracket, chandelier, or sconce, carved elaborately, and usually found on a wall or projecting from a base.

Glare: The sensation produced by luminance within the visual field that is sufficiently greater than the luminance to which the eyes are adapted to cause annoyance, discomfort, or loss in visual performance and visibility.

Glass: A mixture of silica and some alkali resulting in a substance hard, usually brittle, a poor conductor of heat, and possed of a singular luster which, as it resembles the brilliancy of no other common substance, is known by the name of vitreous or glassy luster. The most common kinds of glass are made by fusing together some ordinary form of silica, such as sand, with a sodium salt or some compound of potassium replacing the sodium either wholly or in part, and sometimes with lead. There is no formula of universal application. Moreover, some varieties of glass contain ingredients which are kept secret by the maker, or are compounded in a way which is kept secret. The different kinds of glass in use in architectural practice are: (1) Clear glass in sheets more or less perfectly transparent and including ordinary window glass and plate glass. Under this head come the various modern varieties of glass whose surface is deliberately roughened or ridged or furrowed or pressed in patterns with the purpose of reducing its transparency and allowing it to transmit light while shutting off the view of what may be beyond. (2) Glass in small tesserae or in the tiles of moderate size, usually opaque and very commonly colored. These are used for mosaic of the ordinary fashion, as in flooring and in the adornment of walls and vaults. The tiles are usually cast in one piece, in this resembling plate glass; and it is easy to produce very interesting bas reliefs and also inlaid patterns of great beauty, which may be complete in each tile or may require many tiles to complete the design. Such work was common among the Romans, who lined rooms with glass as freely as with marble. The tesserae, however, are more commonly cut from large sheets by steel tools. The tesserae are sometimes gilded, and so prepared to give to a mosaic picture a background or partial decoration in gold, by making the glass tessera in two parts, laying a piece of gold leaf between the two, and uniting the

whole by heat. (3) Glass in sheets colored throughout its mass and used chiefly for decorative windows. (4) Glass in sheets, flashed, as it is called; that is to say, colored by means of a finer coating of deep colored glass on one or on both sides. This device is used for colors which would be sombre if the whole substance were colored as in pot metal. The deep reds are the colors usually so treated. This also is used for decorative windows. Both the third and fourth kinds of glass are modified in many ways, by the addition of an opaline tinge by the use of arsenic or other chemicals. The opalescent quality, when applied to otherwise uncolored glass, may be described as clouded with a whitish gray opacity, which, however, shows by transmitted light a ruddy spark. In the manufacture of glass for windows of great cost and splendor, it has been found that such opalescent glass, when it has received strong and rich color in addition to the opaline quality, is capable of more perfect harmony, tint with tint, or of a more harmonious contrast, color with color, than if the opaline character had not been given to it. (5) Glass cast in solid prisms, and in prismatic and pyramidal shapes, for the purpose of being set in metal frames and used for vault lights. (6) Glass in the body of which some foreign substance is introduced. This may be done with purely decorative effect, as by the artists of the Roman imperial epoch in vessels of considerable thickness and mass, and this has been imitated by the modern Venetian glassworkers. Wire glass is made on a similar plan for purposes of safety from fire. (7) Soluble glass.

Glass, corrugated: That of which at least one face is ridged; but the term is usually confined to glass which is ridged on each face, the whole substance of the glass being bent into wavelike corrugations exactly as in the case of corrugated metal, the valley on one side forming the ridge on the other.

Glass blowing: The process of forming molten glass into useful objects. The process uses blowing and forming as opposed to molding.

Glass, crown: That which is made by the blowing tube, which produces a bulb-shaped mass which, transferred to the pontil, is revolved rapidly until it suddenly opens out into a circular plate. The glass so produced is often streaky and of unequal thickness. This peculiarity, which has caused the abandonment of crown glass for ordinary window glass, has caused its use in

producing partly opaque and richly colored glass for modern windows; but the sheets made in this way are usually of small size.

Glass, flint: A composition of white sand, potash, niter, and a large amount of red lead, in fact, half as much red lead as all the other above-named ingredients together, to which mass is added cullet, as in the case of plate glass. This glass is not used in strictly architectural work. It is very soft, and scratches easily. It has, however, extraordinary refractive power, and on this account is used for imitation jewelry of all sorts. In this way it enters into architectural decoration, not only in windows, but in the jewelled frames of altarpieces and similar decorative appliances. Flint glass with a still greater amount of red lead is called stress, and is the substance commonly used under the name of paste for mock diamonds.

Glass, ground: Glass of which the surface has been roughened, properly by grinding, or more usually by acid, by the sand blast, or in some similar way, the purpose of the operation being to make it untransparent.

Glass, iridescent: A common translucent glass of some kind, the surface of which has received, by artificial means an iridescence like that of a soap bubble. The ancient Roman and Greek and other glass, especially that found buried in the earth, has an iridescence which comes from a slow process of decomposition. The sheet of glass gradually resolves itself into thin films, and the iridescence is thus a natural result like that in a metallic ore. The iridescent glass is supposed to be made in imitation of this, but it does not resemble it very strongly.

Glass, jealous: Glass depolished or otherwise finished so as to let light pass while it has lost its transparency.

Glass, marbleized: Glass in which the surface is marked by small irregular veins, indicating the places where the glass has been deliberately shattered by plunging into water while hot and then remelted.

Glass, plate: A compound of white sand, sodium carbonate, lime, and either alumina or manganese peroxide, together with a quantity-almost equal to the mass of the above materials--of cullet, or old window glass broken up for remelting. The plate glass is then a solid casting made by pouring the

melted metal upon a flat table of cast iron upon which a castiron roller of the same length as the table's width moves from end to end. The movement of the roller, which rests upon ridges at the sides of the table, fixes the thickness of the plate, and bubbles or other flaws are snatched from the semiliquid mass by pincers. The perfect evenness of the surface and the high polish, upon which, after the purity of the piece, the unequalled transparency and brilliancy of plate glass depend, are obtained by careful grinding and polishing on both sides. Rough plate glass, used for parts of floors, is cast very thick, and its upper surface is left as it cools, neither face being polished.

Glass, prismatic: A glass of which one surface is smooth, while the other is marked by ridges of prismatic section; distinguished from ribbed and corrugated glass by the sharp-edged character of the ridges. This glass may be so made and so fixed in windows that daylight passing through it may be refracted horizontally, or nearly so, and may in this way illuminate a very large internal space.

Glass, ribbed: Glass which has at least one surface ridged or ribbed. The term is usually confined to that which has only one surface so marked, to distinguish it from corrugated glass.

Glass, sheet: Glass produced by blowing into a cylinder which is constantly increased in size, and which is then split lengthwise by a cutter. Being then heated afresh, it falls open by its own weight, the sheet so produced being generally about 3 feet by 4 feet in size. It is rubbed smooth with some soft material, formerly by a piece of partially charred wood. When sheet glass is highly polished, it is sometimes called picture glass, and sometimes, when it is deceptively clear and smooth, patent plate glass.

Glass, stained: Glass which is colored either in its whole mass (pot metal) or by means of flashing, or by means of an applied stain. The only perfectly successful stain is that which gives a yellow, which, coming into use toward the close of the fifteenth century, caused a sudden change in decorative windows throughout the north of Europe. The crimson of flash glass is produced by certain oxides of copper, and by a mixture of gold with oxide of tin. Blue in many different shades, green, purple, etc., are produced by the use of cobalt, though other chemicals are sometimes combined

with it. Manganese gives a dark purple glass, approaching black, which can be brought to almost complete opacity by means of the depth of color alone, thus giving to the worker in colored glass great results in the way of gradation.

Glass, wire: Glass which has a continuous network of wire enclosed in the solid mass. A plate of this glass may bear a very great heat, as of a conflagration, without losing its consistency altogether, although its translucency may be destroyed, and it may crack.

Glaze: (A) To furnish with glass, as a window sash or a door. The term glazed is used more especially to describe the presence or use of glass in a place where it is not uniformly put, as a glazed door, the more common phrase for which in the trade is a sash door. On the other hand, the phrase glazed sash means commonly machine-made window sash with the glass in place ready for delivery, the common way of supplying both sash and glass to a new building. It is only the large lights of plate glass, as for show windows, which are brought to the building without being first fitted to their sash. (B) To give (to anything) a polish or glassy surface; in this sense rare in the building trades, except in ceramics; thus, glazed tile is commonly used in contradistinction to unglazed (i.e. mat or rough surface) tile.

Glazing: A transparent wash or stain used over a dry coat of paint.

Glow: Visible, flameless combustion of the solid phase of a material.

Glue block: A wood block, usually triangular in cross-section, securely glued to an angular joint between two members, for greater glue bond area.

Glue down: The installation process used to adhere carpets down to the floor, on stairs, or walls.

Glued, securely: The bonding of two members with an adhesive forming a tight joint with no visible delamination at the lines of application.

Gobelins: The Gobelin brothers established a dye factory which was later bought by Louis XIV. Furniture and upholstery were produced and, later, tapestries.

Godroon: A convex rounded ornament, differing from a unit of Reeding in not having parallel sides and uniform section throughout.

Commonly it has one end rounded and the other tapering to a point. The term is more properly used for silverware or the like than in architectural practice.

Golden section: A classical proportion. It is defined as a line cut in such a way that the smaller section is to the greater as the greater is to the whole. It was considered a fundamental and divinely given design principal in the Renaissance.

Gold leaf: Gold beaten very thin. It is customary to discriminate between gold foil, which is in sheets as thick as some kinds of paper, and gold leaf, of which it may be said, following the encyclopedias, that an ounce of gold may be beaten out to cover 300 or 400 square feet. The cost of gilding is therefore not largely in the value of the metal used.

Gouache: A painting style using opaque pigments made from watercolors and zinc white.

Governing codes: Codes which are applicable to a project. These include federal and local codes.

Grade: Unless otherwise noted, this term means Woodwork Institute of California Grade Rules, either Economy, Custom, Premium, Utility,

Deluxe, Supreme, or Laboratory. When these terms are used, they mean W.I.C. grade unless otherwise noted.

Grain: (A) An embossed design impressed on a wallcovering. (B) The fibers in wood and their direction, size, arrangement, appearance or quality. When severed, the annual growth rings become quite pronounced and the effect is referred to as grain. (C) The fibers of wood taken together; the fibrous or strongly marked longitudinal texture of wood in which the sheaves of the sap vessels, all running one way, cause a marked distinction between the character of wood if cut crosswise or lengthwise of the log. Blocks for wood engraving are cut across the grain, but in nearly all other careful workmanship the end grain is avoided, and a perhaps excessive care is shown by modern carpenters and joiners never to allow this end grain (that is to say, the texture of the wood as shown when cut across) to be seen. Even in wood when cut in the direction of the grain, that is, lengthwise, there is a difference in the adhesiveness of the parts. Accordingly as a log is cut into parts in the direction or nearly in the direction of the radii of one section of the log considered as a circle, the wood will be found tougher and less liable to split. It is well known that a log allowed to dry naturally will be found checked, or divided deeply by checks. If, then, parts are taken out of a log in such a way that the broad surfaces of these parts go in the direction of these checks, those parts will have little or no tendency to split. Advantage is taken of these circumstances to saw wood quartering, as it is called; the wood specially treated in this way being oak, on account of the open character of its grain. The term is used also to indicate the pattern or veining caused by the irregularity of the arrangement of the sap vessels and fibers. This, in some woods, is of great beauty, and it often happens that a knot, a part of the root, or even one of those curious warts or protuberances which are sometimes found projecting from the trunk of a large old tree, contains wood of a very beautiful pattern. These are called burls. The finest and most precious pieces of this kind are commonly sawed into thin veneers, which are then used by gluing them to thicker pieces of inferior wood. (D) The direction the fibers of a paper run as it is manufactured. It affects surface, directional patterns, folding, tear qualities and dimensional stability.

Grain: To produce, by means of painting, an imitation, more or less close, of the natural grain of wood. The process is chiefly one of wiping, with a cloth held firmly upon the end of a stick, narrow bands in freshly laid paint; these bands showing light in contrast with the darker and thicker paint left on either side. If, for instance, paint the color of walnut is laid over a lighter priming, a skilled grainer will use his wiping tool with greater or less pressure, as he wishes to produce broader and paler or narrower and darker stripes. These stripes, kept close together and nearly parallel, constitute graining of the simplest kind. But the process in the more elaborate patterns is similar to this.

Grain character: A varying pattern produced by cutting through growth rings, exposing various layers. It is most pronounced in veneer cut tangentially or rotary.

Grain, combed or rift: Lmber or veneer that is obtained by cutting at an angle of about 15 degrees off of the quartered position. Twenty-five percent (25%) of the exposed surface area of each piece of veneer may contain medullary ray flake.

Grain figure: The pattern produced in a wood surface by annual growth rings, rays, knots, or deviations from natural grain, such as interlocked and wavy grain, and irregular coloration.

Grain, flat: (FG.) lumber or veneer is a piece sawn or sliced approximately parallel to the annual growth rings so that some or all of the rings form an angle of less than 45 degrees with the surface of the piece.

Grain, slashed: (S.G.) same as flat grain.

Grain, mixed: (M.G.) is any combination of Vertical or Flat Grain in the same member.

Grain, vertical: (V.G.) lumber or veneer is a piece sawn or sliced at approximately right angles to the annual growth rings so that the rings form an angle of 45 degrees or more with the surface of the piece.

Grain, quartered: is a method of sawing or slicing to bring out certain figures produced by the medullary or pith rays, which are especially conspicuous in oak. The log is flitched in several different ways to allow the cutting of the veneer in a radial direction.

Grandfather chair: See wing chair.

Grass cloth: See wallcoverings.

Greek key: A hook shaped square form that is in a geometrical repetition of fretwork patterns.

Greenfield: Flexible metallic tubing for the protective enclosure of electric wires.

Greige Goods: (Pronounced "gray goods") Undyed carpet or other textile materials.

Grille: A grating of metal or wood that is used as a barrier or as decoration.

Grinning: Visibility of carpet backing through the face, often between two adjoining tuft rows. May be caused by low pile yarn weight, off-gauge tufting machine parts, tuft row deflection, inadequate blooming of pile yarn, or installation over sharp curves such as stair nosings.

Grisaille: Painting shades of grey with a monochromatic style.

Groove: A narrow continuous sinking, usually of the same width and depth throughout. Grooves are worked on the edges of boards and planks for the purpose of making tongued and grooved flooring and sheathing. Rectangular slot of three surfaces cut paralleled with the grain of the wood.

Gros point: A technique of cross-stitch with wool stitched on canvas.

Grotesque: A Roman wall ornament made up of sphinxed, foliage, medallions, etc. executed in stucco or paint.

Ground: (I.) Anything used to fix a limit or to regulate the thickness or projection of the more permanent or of exterior finished work. The term is generally used in the plural; thus, grounds in ordinary building are pieces of wood secured to the jamb of a doorway, as in a brick wall, or to the base of a stud partition, to stop the plastering at the edge and to determine its thickness, and to these grounds the wooden trim may be nailed, or the grounds may be removed. Also, any strip secured to a wall, and more or less embedded in the plaster, to furnish a nailing, as to secure a wooden mantel, heavy trim, or the like.

Ground: (II.) (A) In painting, the surface upon which ornaments and the like are relieved, corresponding nearly to background in relief sculpture, and to the French *champ*. (B) (Used attributively) having to do with the ground or background;

thus, ground color is the color used for the ground as in definition A.

Ground color: The background color against which the top colors create the pattern of figure in the design.

Grounded: A conductor that is in contact with or connected to the earth.

Ground floor: Properly, that floor of a building which is most nearly on a level with the surrounding surface of the ground. By extension, same as Ground Story.

Grounding: Connection of electric components to earth for safety.

Ground line: (G.L.) The intersection of the ground plane and the picture plane. It is used as a measuring line.

Ground plane: (G.P). This is the floor or ground of the scene. All vertical measures refer to this.

Group relamping: Relamping of a group of luminaries at one time to reduce relamping labor costs.

Gueridon: (French) Small ornamental stand.

Guilloche: A furniture design of carving or inlay composed of curves or rosettes. A molding enrichment made in the form of plaited interlacing bands.

Gully: The predetermined space left between the anchored tackless strips and the adjacent wall. Also known as pinch in.

Gum, gumwood: A wood that is white to grey-green in color and used on low-grade cabinet making. It often warps but finishes well.

Gusset: A triangular piece of metal to serve as a brace in the angle formed by two intersecting members of a framework, either to stiffen the connection, or as a support of one of the members.

H

Hadley chest: A seventeenth century chest with front sunken panels, two drawers and a hinged top. The chest was produced in Hadley, Massachusetts and often the owner's initials were carved on it.

Hair: Animal fiber other than wool or silk.

Hair cloth: Fabric made from horsehair or a blend of horsehair, cotton and linen.

Half lap: A joint formed by extending (lapping) the joining part of one member over the joining part of the other member.

Hand-block printing: A technique of printing on cloth which uses patterns engraved or carved on linoleum, metal or wood blocks to transfer patterns of ink or paint.

Hand: The tactile aesthetic qualities of carpets and textiles. Factors determining how carpets feel to the hand include weight, stiffness, fiber type, denier, and density.

Handkerchief table: A table that has a triangular shaped drop-leaf and top.

Handrail: The railing along the side of a stair or steps used to maintain balance while climbing.

Hanging: The art or process of securing in place a door, casement, or shutter, by means of hinges, a sliding sash or the like by means of counterpoise and cords, or sliding doors when these are supported from overhead or from the side by means of sheaves or rollers of any kind.

Hardboard: A generic term for a panel manufactured primarily from interfleted ligno-cellulose fibers consolidated under heat and pressure in a hot press and conforming to the requirement of PS 58-74.

Hard finish: Fine white plaster which, when used, forms the last coat of a piece of plastering.

Hard-paste: A type of clay pottery made with a base of kaolin.

Harness: Part of a weaving loom comprising the frames holding the heddles through which the warp yarns pass, and used to raise and lower them to form the shed in which the shuttles move to insert fill yarn.

Harpsichord: An instrument that is similar to the piano. It has strings that are plucked by leather or quill points connected with the keys.

Harvard chair: A seventeenth century armchair with three legs.

Harvest table: A dining room table with drop leaves.

Hasp: A fastener for a door, lid, or the like, usually in the form of a plate or bar of metal hinged at one end, and with a slot or opening to receive a staple. A padlock, or in default of this a pin of wood or the like, being passed through the staple, the door, etc., is held fast.

Hassock: A cushion or footstool used to kneel or sit.

Haviland: Porcelain dishes made for everyday use.

Headroom: The clear space allowed above a flight of steps or a floor, platform, or the like, so that a person passing will have abundant room. The space should be sufficient to remove all sense of annoyance from the nearness of the floor or flight of stairs above. Thus, where stairs are arranged, one flight above another, 7 feet in the clear vertically is the least space that should be allowed. As soon as a stair and its surroundings assume some architectural character, the headroom must be much greater than this, and its proper distribution is an important consideration in planning. By extension, the term is loosely applied to any space allowed vertically for a given purpose; as when an attic room is said to have 4 feet headroom at the low side nearest the eaves.

hearth: A piece of floor prepared to receive a fire; whether in the middle of a room, as in primitive times, the smoke being allowed to escape through openings in the roof; or, as in later times, the floor of a fireplace in the modern sense. The hearth of ancient times was sometimes raised above the floor, and then had often a low rim around it; and sometimes sunk beneath it, forming the bottom of a shallow pit. In either case it might be fitted with certain permanent holders for wood representing the dogs or andirons of later times. Some cooking hearths, as in Pompeii, are raised a foot or more above the floor, and are built of masonry, with an arched opening at one side in which fuel might have been kept. The hearth, then, includes properly the entire floor from the back lining of the fireplace to the outermost edge of the incombustible material. In builder's usage, however, it is very often customary not to include in the term the rougher flooring, as of hard brick, which is enclosed between the actual cheeks of the recess made in the wall or chimney breast. According to this custom, the hearth, or, as it might be called, the outer hearth, is usually a slab of slate, soapstone, marble or other fairly resistant material, which is placed outside of and beyond the fireplace proper. The mantelpiece in modern usage generally rests upon it, as do the fender and the front feet of the basket grate, or other fittings. A flooring of tile sometimes replaces the slab of stone. Whatever the material of the hearth, it is usually supported upon a flat arch of brickwork which often is built between the trimmers of the floor below; the area in front of the fireplace.

Heart-shaped chair: A chair whose back looks like two hearts intertwined.

Heartwood: The wood formed at the interior or heart of a tree. It is quite free from sap,-the more so as the tree becomes older,-of finer and more compact and even grain, and therefore harder. It is usually considered better for general use than the outer portion of the trunk which contains the sap, and is,

hence, known as sapwood. The latter has comparatively little strength and is more liable to rapid decay.

Heat Extraction: The process of removing heat from a luminaire by passing return air through the lamp cavity.

Heather: A multicolor effect provided by blending fibers of different colors prior to spinning carpet yarn.

Heat melt bonded: This term refers to those fabrics in which a bonding agent has been used between the primary and secondary backs of a tufted carpet. The material replaces conventional latex. Since the thermoplastic material is applied in a molten state, it thoroughly penetrates the portion of face yarn between the primary and secondary back. The resulting bond between the components is exceptionally strong, producing an outstanding tuft bind as well as ravel resistance and secondary backing adhesion.

Heat resistance test: A sample of the laminated plastic approximately 12" x 12" glued to substratum for a minimum of 21 days shall be used for this test. A hot air gun rated at 14 amperes, 120 volts, with a nozzle temperature of 500⁰ F or 274⁰ C shall be directed at the surface of the test panel. A thermometer set at the panel surface shall register 356° F or 180° C for an exposure time of 5 minutes. The formation of a blister or void between the overlay and the substratum shall constitute a failure of the adhesive. A metal straight edge shall be used to determine if a blister has occurred. This determination shall be made within 30 seconds of heat removal.

Heat setting: Process for stabilization of carpet yarns by exposure to heat. Conventional autoclave heat-setting treats yarns in relaxed skein configuration with pressurized steam, usually at temperatures in the 240-300° F range, often 270° F for nylon. Some continuous heat-setting machines employ dry heat. The principal benefits are twist retention in plied yarns in cut-pile carpet and general stabilization of yarn configuration.

Heddle: Part of a weaving loom comprising one of the sets of parallel wires, blades, or cords (often with eyelets in their centers through which warp yarns pass) that with their mounting compose the harness used to guide warp threads and raise and lower them in weaving.

Heddle frame: Part of a weaving loom in which the heddles are mounted.

Helix: A spiral motif, for example the inner spiral of the volute on a Corinthian capital.

Hepplewhite: A style of furniture that was characterized by shield and oval backs. Satinwood and mahogany were the woods most often used.

Heraldry: The art and science of the herald; the only branch of which at all connected with architecture is the determination and marshalling of arms.

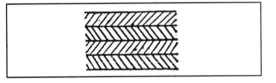

Herringbone work: Decoratively assembled stone, brick, wood, marquetry, etc., assembled with the components laid diagonally rather than horizontally. Alternate courses alternate, thereby forming a zigzag pattern.

Hessian: Plain woven jute fabric with approximately equal numbers of warp and fill yarns per unit dimension.

Hex sign: A sign in the shape of a circle with a six-pointed star inside. It is most often seen on Pennsylvania German buildings and confers either bad or good luck. They are used as a decorative folk motif.

Highboy: A tall chest of drawers that sits on a low chest.

High density foam: Attached carpet cushion made from compounded natural and/or synthetic latex foam having a minimum density of 17 pounds per cubic foot and a minimum weight of 38 ounces per square yard.

High Intensity Discharge (HID) lamp: A discharge lamp in which the light producing arc is stabilized by wall temperature, and the arc tube has a bulb wall loading in excess of three watts per square centimeter. HID lamps include groups of lamps known as mercury, metal halide, and high pressure sodium.

High low: Multilevel carpet style comprising high and low loop pile areas or high cut-pile and low loop areas. The latter is also called a cut and loop style.

High-low cocktail table: A table that can raise in height.

High output fluorescent lamp: Operates at 800 or more milliamperes for higher light output than standard fluorescent lamp (430MA).

High Pressure Laminated Plastic: Laminated thermosetting decorative sheets intended for decorative purposes. The sheets consist essentially of layers of a fibrous sheet material, such as paper, impregnated with a thermosetting condensation resin and consolidated under heat and pressure. The top layers have a decorative color or a printed design. The resultant product has an attractive exposed surface which is durable and resistant to damage from abrasion and mild alkalies, acids and solvents, meeting the requirements of the National Electrical Manufacturers Association (NEMA) LD 3-80, or latest revision thereof.

High pressure laminating: Plastics are put into a hopper and fed through a heating chamber. The material is softened into a fluid form. There is a nozzle which abuts an opening into a mold, the fluid is forced through with pressure, and is then cooled and ejected from the press.

High Pressure Sodium (HPS) Lamp: High intensity discharge (HID) lamp in which light is produced by radiation from sodium vapor. Includes clear and diffuse-coated lamps.

Hinge: A connection used to attach and support a member or structure so that it may be movable as about a pivot; as a door, sash, table leaf, or the like. The movable member may be hung by means of the hinge to a fixed support as a frame or jamb, or to another movable piece. In its common form, a hinge consists of two flaps or leaves of metal, each of which has one edge bent about a pin, wholly or in part; such a portion, or both together, forming the knuckle. The pin thus forms a pivot about which one flap is free to turn when the other is permanently secured. The simplest form of hinge may be formed by a hook permanently fixed, as the stationary member, and a ring secured to the movable member.

Historic preservation: The interior and exterior preserved for historic value.

Hole: Applies to holes from any cause. A pin hole is approximately 1/16" in diameter.

Home office: A space in the den or a separate room where work from the office can be done.

Homespun: Coarse woven fabric made of bulky yarns.

Honeysuckle ornament: A design with honeysuckle flowers and leaves in a cluster.

Hood-molding: Molding projecting above a doorway or window to shed rain.

Hoof foot: A design carved in the shape of an animal's hoof.

Hooked rug: A rug made by hooking strips of yarn or wool through a burlap or canvas backing.

Horizon line: The line that runs parallel to the ground line and intersects the center or the view on the picture plane. This corresponds to the eye-level of the observer. In interior perspective it is usually five or five and one-half feet above the ground line.

Horn furniture: Furniture that is made from the horns or antlers of deer or elk etc.

Horsehair: Hair from the tail or the mane of a horse made into fabric.

Hot melt: Adhesive material sometimes used for laminating secondary backing to tufted carpet; also used as the adhesive component of carpet seaming tape. Hot melt adhesives are compounded from thermoplastic polymers and plastics. They may be melted and solidified repeatedly by application of heat.

Hot melt bonded carpet: A fabric in which a thermoplastic adhesive is applied with heat to bond the secondary back to the primary back of the carpet.

Hot melt seams: Also known as Heat Bonding. In practice the backs of the edges to be seamed are positioned to lie over a centrally located continuous length of a seaming tape coated by the tape manufacturer with a thermoplastic adhesive. The adhesive is activated (melted) with the application of a slowly moving iron from which this seaming process derives its term, hot melt. The two backs are pressed down into the melted adhesive which is then allowed to cool, completing the seam.

Housing: (A) A groove, recess, or the like, cut or formed in one piece, usually of wood, for the insertion of the edge or end of another. (B) Any light, houselike structure, as for a temporary shelter.

Huche: (French) Hutch or chest.

Hunt table: An eighteenth century table with dropleaves used as a bar.

Hurricane glass or lamp: A glass cylinder that is open at both ends and is placed on a candle to prevent it from extinguishing.

Husk garland: A tapering festoon of nutshells.

Hutch: A seventeenth century cabinet with doors, shelves and storage space, used to display dishes. It was originally used to store clothing or food.

I

Imari ware: See Arita porcelain.

Incandescent lamp: A lamp in which light is produced by a filament heated to incandescence by an electric current.

Incised work: That which is done by cutting into a surface. This, if carried through the piece of metal so as to be open on both sides, is usually called pierced work, also by the French term *A Jour*; more rarely by the Italian term *A Giorno*. Lettering of any sort cut into the metal is properly called inscription; and a piece of lettering an inscription. The term incised work is then limited in practice to decorative sculpture in which a flat surface is adorned with a pattern sunk beneath it, or with a pattern left in relief, while the background is cut away. If this pattern is rounded and modelled into sculpture, it becomes relief. If the pattern, or the cut away parts which surround the pattern, are filled in with some other material, the term used is generally inlay or inlaid work; but it is also said that a pattern is incised and then filled in with mastic, or other soft material.

Inclination: Slope of any kind; especially in building that has to do with decorative effect as contrasted with Batter, which is the slope of walls made thicker at the base for strength, or in a fortification for defence; any slope which is more commonly applied to a roof or ramp of a staircase. Thus, the axes of a Doric column in Greek work are found to have been generally inclined to the vertical, and in medieval work, walls and pillars are continually set with an incline. The angle of inclination is that which a roof, a ramp, or other essentially sloping member makes, either with the horizon, or with a vertical plane. It is rare that this is estimated by builders in terms of mathematical science, as in so many degrees and minutes. More commonly it is estimated by the horizontal dimensions compared with the vertical dimensions. Thus a carpenter will say that the inclination of his roof is three (horizontal) to two (vertical).

Indoor outdoor carpet: A term synonymous with outdoor carpet.

Industry foundation: An organization that represents manufacturers who provide products and services for interior designers.

Inflatable furniture: Furniture which is filled with gas or liquid.

Inlaid work: Decoration by inserting a piece of one material within an incision or depression made for it in another piece of material. The term is usually confined to a combination in this way of hard materials, as black marble in white, or, as in some marble pavements in Florentine mosaic, etc., of many different colored materials on a plain background. It is extended to mean incised work filled with paste which becomes hard. Inlays in wood, if Italian in their design or their origin, are called *tarsia* or *intarsiatura*. Surfaces made up of many small parts fitted together are properly mosaic, no matter how large the pieces are, because in this case, as in the fine mosaics of a vault, there is no continuous and solid background in which the other pieces are inlaid. A patch of mosaic may, however, be inlaid upon a larger surface.

Inlay: The process of laying a material such as bone or pewter into metal or wood.

Inside finish: In the United States, the fittings, such as doors and door trims, window trims, shutters, door-saddles and the like, dadoes or wall lining with wood, marble, or tile; sometimes also mantelpieces and even sideboards, presses, or dressers if put up permanently. The term is most commonly used for the woodwork of ordinary dwelling houses and business buildings, but is extended to the most elaborate and permanent work.

Installation: The assembly of a manufactured or other building component or system on site and the process of fixing in position for use as a building component or system.

Instant start fluorescent lamp: A fluorescent lamp designed for starting by a high voltage without preheating of the electrodes.

Intaglio: A design that is stamped or cut under the surface of a hard material.

Intarsia: A mosaic of colored woods. Small sections of wood that are inlaid and used to create a mosaic.

Inverse square law: The law stating that the illuminance at a point on a surface varies directly with the intensity of a point source, and inversely as the square of the distance between the source and the point. If the surface at the point is normal to the direction of the incident light, the law is expressed by $fc=cp/d^2$.

Ironstone china: China that was first manufactured in 1813 and was made with the slag of ironstone.

Ironwork: Decorative or structural elements made from wrought iron.

Isolux chart: A series of lines plotted on any appropriate set of coordinates, each line connecting all the points on a surface having the same illumination.

Isometric projection: A drawing showing an object in three dimensions. A plan is established with lines at an equal angle to the horizontal, usually 30 degrees. Vertical lines remain vertical. All lines are drawn to scale. Diagonals and curves are distorted.

Italian furniture: Furniture characterized by six different styles. The Pre-Renaissance (1100-1400) style modeled Byzantine and Gothic art. The Quatrocento (1400-1500) style had very classic and simple details. The Cinquecento (1500-1600) style was dominated by rich and elaborate carvings. The Baroque (1650-1700) style was characterized by exaggerated and ornate designs. The Settecento (1700-1750) style had lavish but elegant designs. The other styles duplicated Directoire, Louis XVI, and Hepplewhite styles.

J

Jacaranda: See palisander.

Jacquard system: (A) The mechanism on a Wilton loom that is activated by prepunched cards to select the desired color of yarn to form part of the design on the pile surface of the carpet. (B) Fabric made on a Jacquard loom. It produces a figured design similar to brocade or damask.

Jalousie: A structure of slender uprights and crosspieces, either a lattice, or, more usually, a set of louver boards, the whole so arranged as to admit air freely and a subdued light, while excluding the view of persons outside. A window may be filled with these slats, or a balcony enclosed by them on every side. Some panels may swing on hinges, while other are fixed. In tropical climates, town houses are often completely enclosed with jalousies for all above the ground story; and these wholly replace walls and glazed windows for at least a part of the external enclosure. Sometimes, also, glazed sashes are inserted in the wall of jalousies, for the purpose of affording more light and some view out of doors during heavy rains, when the hinged panels can hardly be opened. By extension, the term is applied to movable window shades, and especially to those which are made of slats pierced for cords, and movable upon them so that by pulling the cords the slats can be turned easily at different angles, and can also be brought together at the top so as to leave the window unobstructed.

Japan: A furniture polish that was used to imitate the appearance of lacquer in the seventeenth and eighteenth centuries.

Japanese painted screens: These were not only used as partitions but considered as works of art. They were painted with flowers, birds or mythological subjects and were covered with leather or silk.

Jardiniere: (French) A flower pot or stand that was decorated and had four legs and a metal-lined well.

Jasper ware: An eighteenth century stoneware that can be stained and is close grained.

Jenny Lind style: A nineteenth style of furniture with spool arms and leg turnings.

Jig: A woodworking making tool used as a pattern or guide.

Jigsaw: A saw that has a long small blade used in cutting fretwork or latticework.

Joinery: Joiner's work; the interior fittings of dwellings, etc., dadoes, door trim, and the like. The term would be more appropriate for the entire decorative woodwork of interiors than for cabinet work, but has nearly become obsolete, at least in the United States.

Joint: (A) Any beam intended primarily for the construction or support of a floor, ceiling, or the like, and horizontal or nearly so. By extension, a sleeper as used for the support of a wooden floor over a masonry or fireproof floor. (B) In the United States, a stud or piece of scantling about three inches by four inches in size. (C) The place at which two parts, or pieces, meet, and sometimes unite; the surfaces so brought together considered collectively; also the space between two such faces, which may or may not be filled with a cohesive material to unite the two parts; hence, the mass of cohesive material so placed. Any two pieces brought into more or less close contact form a joint between them. A wall built of stones without the use of mortar is said to have dry joints; that is, that the interstices, or spaces between the stones, are not filled with mortar. An architect's specifications may call for joints of stonework to be dressed in a certain manner, which requirement would apply to the faces which it is intended to bring into contact. Again, it may be required that brickwork is to be laid in certain mortar with 3/8" joints, such stipulation referring to the thickness of the mass of mortar between the bricks. Again, two timbers may be framed by a mortice and tenon joint, the term in such case being applied to the several contiguous surfaces, together with the parts immediately connected. In connecting lead pipes end to end, the solder forms a homogeneous mass completely enveloping the butting ends, the whole assemblage being known as a wiped joint.

Joint, lap: A type of joint in which one piece of wood overlaps another and is held together with glue or nails.

Junction box: A metal box in which circuit wiring is spliced. It may also be used for mounting luminaries, switches or receptacles.

Jute: A natural cellulosic fiber made from certain plants of the linden family which grow in warm climates such as found in India and

Bangladesh. Jute yarns are used for utility fabrics, woven carpet construction (backing) yarns and twine. Woven jute fabrics are used in tufted carpet as primary and secondary carpet backing. The latter are similar to burlap fabrics commonly used for carpet wrap and sewn burlap bags.

K

K'ang: A Chinese platform used for a sleeping area or to place furniture, usually covered with woven mats.

Kakemono: A Japanese scroll that is painted or inscribed and made with silk paper.

Kapok: Stuffing used in mattresses and pillows that comes from the silk-cotton tree.

Kas or Kast: A seventeenth century armoire with fruit designs or a finish and panelled doors.

Kerman or Kirman rug: A Persian rug with soft colors and a border with an elaborate pattern.

Key: (A) An instrument for fastening and unfastening a lock; capable of being inserted or withdrawn, and when withdrawn, leaving the lock incapable of being opened or shut except by violence. The principal parts of an ordinary key are as follows: Bow-the enlargement at one end of the shank whereby the key is turned by the fingers. Bit-the lug at the end of the shank which fits into the lock and raises the tumbler and turns the bolt of the lock. The bit is cut and grooved to fit itself to the various wards and levers of the lock. Shank-the shaft connecting the bow and bit. In the East, keys are commonly of wood, and a series of metal pins set into the wooden bar of the key can be adjusted to holes on the lock, thus raising tumblers and allowing the latch to be withdrawn. The metal keys of the Middle Ages and the succeeding centuries were often the medium of exquisite decoration, not merely in the graceful and picturesque proportion of the parts of the key proper, bit, shank, and bow; but also in the way of delicate chasing and even elaborate inlay of other materials than iron. Locks and keys of extraordinary beauty have been preserved when the wooden chests which they were made for have disappeared, and these are among the jewels of our collections of ornamental art. (B) A wedge, or a tapering piece or member, used singly, or in pairs, as a means of drawing two parts together and tightly securing them when it is forced into an aperture prepared for the purpose; or as a means of holding two members or surfaces apart; hence, a member for a similar purpose, whether so shaped or not, designed for insertion into recessed in two or more adjoining parts, and commonly secured in place by wedges or keys of the specified form. Thus a key may be used instead of a cleat for securing together a number of boards edge to edge; and will be itself formed of a tapering board forced into a corresponding groove cut across the assembled boards; the cross section of such a key and its corresponding groove has usually a dovetail shape, flaring inward, for greater security. A common use of keys is in heavy framing, as in forming a scarf joint, or assembling the parts of a truss. For the last purpose, a key is commonly of iron, and known as a cotter, and used in connection with a gib, or gibs. (C) In plastering, or similar work, that part of the plastic material which enters into the interstices, or clings to the rough surface, of the backing or prepared support; and by its adherence sustains the coat of mortar, or like material. Thus, the first coat of plaster applied to lathing forms a key when pressed through the spaces arranged for it; and this coat being scratched or roughened enables the next coat to form a key.

Kidney table: A desk that has an opened space for the knees and is in the shape of a kidney.

Kilim: A rug that is made of wool and handwoven.

Kiln dried: Lumber dried in a closed chamber in which the removal of moisture is controlled by artificial heat and usually by controlled relative humidity.

Kilowatt-Hour: (KWH) Unit of electrical power consumed over a period of time. KWH=watts/1000 x hours used.

Kitchen: The room in which food is prepared and usually eaten.

Kneehole desk: A desk with draws on either side and an open space for the knees.

Knee kicker: A carpet installation tool consisting of a pinned plate connected to a short section of metal tubing. The end opposite to the plate has a padded cushion which the installer strikes with his knee to stretch carpet which is gripped by the pinned plate. Knee kickers should be used only in areas which are so small that power stretchers cannot be used. In general, adequate stretching of carpet installations cannot be achieved with knee kickers.

Knife case: A container used to hold knives, often decorated.

Knitted carpets: Although the face and back of a knitted carpet is made in one operation like a woven carpet, the method by which this is done is different. The machine uses three sets of needles to loop together the backing yarns, stitching yarns, and the pile yarns, similar to the way hand knitting is done. Then a heavy coat of backing compound is applied to the back to give the carpet added body. Sometimes a preformed secondary back, like those used in tufted carpets, is laminated to give this fabric additional stability. Since the knitting machine uses a single pile yarn, this type of carpet is usually manufactured in a loop pile texture of either solid color or tweed effects. Some knitted fabrics may have textured designs produced by varying the heights of the pile loops. Other knitted fabrics may be fabricated with a plush cut pile or a combination of cut and loop pile but these are relatively rare.

Knob: A rounded projection; in architecture sometimes a piece of utility, as when furnishing the handle to a door lock, or door latch, and sometimes an ornament. In this latter sense the term implied generally the termination of a slender and isolated member.

Knobbing: In stone cutting, a preliminary process; usually the mere knocking off of pieces projecting beyond the required dimensions.

Knocker: A contrivance, generally of metal, to be attached to the outside of an outer door to enable a visitor to announce his presence by means of a knock or light blow. Its essential part is a hammerlike, pivoted arm which is raised and allowed to fall against a plate.

Knock-off: An object that is a copy of something else and is sold at a lower price.

Knotty pine: Pine wood with knots that when cut forms a decorative pattern.

Korean furniture: A style of furniture often with mother-of-pearl inlay, clean lines, and lavishly ornamented.

Kusters dyeing: Continuous dyeing using the kusters dye applicator and range.

L

Labeled: Equipment bearing a label of certification of an approved listing organization.

Label-Stop: An ornamental boss at the beginning and end of a hood-mold.

Lacquer: Properly, a substance made of lac, that is to say, of the substance sold as gum-lac, stick-lac, seed-lac, shell-lac or shellac; but by extension applied also to a varnish made in Oriental countries from the sap of certain plants.

Lacunar: A coffered or panelled ceiling.

Ladder-back chair: A chair that has horizontal pieces of wood on the back to resemble a ladder.

Lalique: A type of French glass that has low-relief designs. The designs are molded, pressed, and then engraved on the glass.

Lambrequin: (French) A valance board for draperies. A frame that surrounds a window and is usually covered in fabric.

Laminate: A product produced by bonding two or more materials. See High Pressure Laminated Plastic.

Laminated: Layer construction of lumber. May be either horizontal or vertical layers securely glued together.

Lamp: An artificial source of light (also a portable luminaire equipped with a cord and plug).

Lamp efficacy: The ratio of lumens produced by a lamp to the watts consumed. Expressed as lumens per watt (LPW).

Lamp Lumen Depreciation: (LLD) Multiplier factor in illumination calculations for reduction in the light output of a lamp over a period of time.

Lampshades: Decorative covers for table and floor lamps and sconces which prevent direct glare from the light source.

Laque: (French) Lacquered.

Latex: A water emulsion of synthetic rubber, natural rubber, or other polymer. In carpet, latex is used for laminating secondary backings to tufted carpet, backcoating carpet and rugs, and for manufacturing foamed cushion.

Almost all carpet latex consists of styrene-butadiene synthetic rubber (SBR) compounded with large quantities of powdered fillers. The latter are most often whiting, which is calcium carbonate.

Latexing: A term used to describe the application of a natural or synthetic latex compound to the back of carpet.

Latex seaming: Also known in the industry as wet seaming. A seaming process that uses a liquid latex adhesive and a tape manufactured for this purpose to join two pieces of carpet together by adhering the tape to the backs of the edges being seamed.

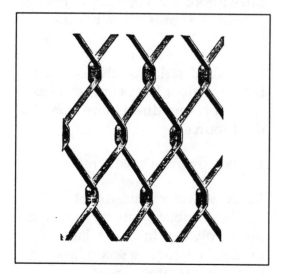

Lath: A strip of metal or wood, generally quite thin and narrow, but often approaching a batten or furring strip in size; a number of which are intended to be secured to beams, studs, and such members for the support of tiles, slates, plaster, and similar finishing materials.

Lath, counter: (A) An intermediate lath or batten interposed between a pair of Gauge Laths. (B) One of a supplementary set; as when laths are nailed across others used as furring.

Lath, gauge: In roofing, one of a number of laths placed by accurate measurement so as to support a tile or slate at the proper points, as at the nail holes.

Lath, metallic: A preparation of metal, usually wrought, rolled, or drawn iron, to receive plastering by having openings which give a good key or hold to the plaster, and which is also capable of being secured to woodwork or metal work in the construction. The most common form has heretofore been a coarse wire netting with the mesh of 3/4" or thereabout, and this is commonly called wire lath.

Lath, wire: Same as metal lath.

Lazy Susan: A circular tray that holds food or condiments that revolves.

Leaf and dart: Ovolo molding enhanced with leaf-like forms alternating with darts.

Leather: A material that comes from the skin of animals. Once the hair is removed the skin is tanned and many different objects are produced. Beginning in the sixteenth century furniture was first upholstered with leather and now everything from purses and shoes to jackets and belts are made from leather.

Leno weave: A woven fabric construction in which paired warp yarns twist around one another between fill yarn picks. It is similar to woven gauze bandage construction. Leno construction renders the yarns relatively immobile within the fabric, making possible very open weaves which are relatively stable. Woven polypropylene secondary backings for tufted carpets are generally of leno weave construction.

Lenox: American china first manufactured in 1889 and considered competitive with European china.

Lens: Used in luminaries to redirect light into useful zones.

Leroy lettering set: A plastic template used to guide a scriber with an ink pen to letter many sizes and styles of type on plans and drawings. This is an excellent way for neat titles. Sets come with as few as three lettering templates and a scribe.

Level loop: A carpet style having all tufts in a loop form and of identical height. May be woven or tufted.

Libbey glass: A nineteenth century glass company specializing in cut glass.

Library steps: Portable steps or free-standing ladder used in a library to retrieve books form high shelves.

Library table: A large table used as a desk or study surface in a library.

Light: In architecture (A) The volume of daylight received in a room, corridor, or the like. The term is often used in composition, as in the subtitle Borrowed Light. By extension, a similar volume of light from an artificial source; as a closet may have a borrowed light from a room lighted by electricity. (B) An opening or medium through which daylight may pass, as a pane (called generally by glaziers and carpenters a light) of glass. More especially the opening between two mullions or window bars in a decorative window, the glass of which is commonly in irregular or other small pieces, hardly called lights in this case. (C) An artificial source of light; a means of providing light, as in the compound or qualified terms gas light, electric light. Thus, in arranging for the lighting of an interior, it may be stipulated that 10 lights be ranged along the cornice on either side. (D) The manner or the nature of the illumination received by a picture or other work of art, or by a wall or ceiling considered as the medium for the display of such work of art. Thus, it may be said that there is no good light for pictures on the east wall. (E) Radiant energy that is capable of exciting the retina and producing a visual sensation. The visible portion of the electromagnetic spectrum extends from about 380 to 770 nm.

Light Loss Factor: (LLF) A factor used in calculating the level of illumination that takes into account such factors as dirt accumulation on luminaire and room surfaces, lamp depreciation, maintenance procedures and atmosphere conditions. See Maintenance Factor.

Light output: Amount of light produced by a light source such as a lamp. The unit most commonly used to measure light output is the lumen.

Limoges: Manufactory of fine china named after the city in France where it is located.

Lincoln rocker: An upholstered rocking chair with a straight back.

Linear perspective: Lines that suggest a three dimensional object on a two dimensional surface and give the illusion of distance.

Linenfold: A decorative element that looks similar to a scroll or folded cloth. Tudor panelling in the form of vertically folded linen.

Linen press: A machine that presses linen between two boards with applied pressure.

Lining: (A) A cushioning material made of felted cattle hair and jute, or rubber or plastic foam, or other materials, used as an underlayment of rugs and carpets. Also known in the industry as cushion or underlay. (B) Material used to cover the interior of anything; hence a member forming the back or internal face of a structure. Seldom used except in special combinations; as jamb lining, window back lining.

Lining paper: (blank stock) Paper that is applied under wallpaper for better adhesion.

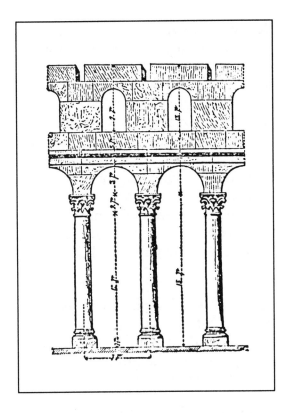

Lintel: A beam or the like over an opening, which carried the weight of the wall above it. It may be of wood, or iron, or of stone. The bearings of its ends on the jambs of the opening must be sufficient to prevent injury from pressure to the material, either of the lintel or of the jamb; and if the opening is very wide, it may be necessary to consider also the strength of the foundations under the jambs, upon which the entire weight above the opening must come.

Lion motif: An ancient Egyptian decorating style used on furniture.

Listed: Equipment or materials or structures included in a list published by an approved listing organization.

Listing agency: An agency which is authorized by the appropriate code enforcement agency to evaluate and approve specific products or systems.

Lit: (French) Bed.

Lit canape: (French) Sofa bed.

Lit d'ange: (French) A bed with a small canopy.

Lit duchesse: (French) A bed with a large canopy.

Lit-a-la-Francaise: (French) A canopy bed that is placed sideways against wall.

Lit-a-la-Polonaise: (French) A bed with pointed canopy.

Lit-a-traverse: (French) A bed without a canopy placed sideways against wall.

Lites: The panes of glass between narrow strips of wood on a window.

Living room: The principal room in which residents gather for social entertainment.

Load-bearing: A wall that is capable of bearing another weight as well as its own.

Local government: Any municipality, county, district or combination thereof comprising a governmental unit.

Local Lighting: Lighting designed to provide illuminance over a relatively small area or confined space without providing any significant general surrounding lighting.

Lock: Interlocking machine joint between two members.

Long life lamps: See Extended Life Lamps.

Loom: Machine which produces woven fabrics. In weaving, lengthwise yarns (warp) are interlaced with yarns (fill), and inserted at right angles to them by the shuttle (or other device such as gripper or rapier).

Loomed carpet (sponge bonded, high density pile): These are terms commonly used to describe a carpet made on a loom originally designed for weaving upholstery fabrics. This loom forms a pile layer of tightly woven low loops without the use of loom wires over a high strength single filling yarn and one ground warp yarn in a staggered diagonal pattern across the width of the pile layer. The back of this pile layer is then coated with an adhesive to which a sponge rubber batter is applied and cured with heat. The pile is usually of nylon although some are made with wool or acrylic pile yarns.

Looper: A tufting machine partially used in tufted carpet production. It is a thin flat metal hook that removes pile yarn from the tufting needle at the bottom of the downstroke.

Loop pile: Carpet style having a pile surface consisting of uncut loops. May be woven or tufted. Also called round wire in woven carpet terminology.

Loose and long: Run to pattern only. Not assembled, nor machined for assembly, nor cut to length. The terms material only and mill run mean the same as loose and long.

Loose seat cushion: A seat cushion which is removable or interchangeable.

Lost wax process: A method of lining a mold with wax then replacing it with bronze to produce an exact copy of the original.

Love seat: A couch that is designed for two people.

Lowestoft porcelain: English porcelain containing bone ash and often decorated in the Chinese style.

Low pressure decorative polyester overlay: Overlays comprised of polyester resin saturated cellulosic sheets thermo-bonded to the particleboard, hardboard, or plywood core. The face overlay shall contain a decorative color or printed design. The other side may have a suitable balance sheet bonded in the same manner. The resultant product has an attractive exposed surface which is durable and resistant to damage from abrasion and mild alkalies, acids and solvents, and meets the requirements of the following standards; National Electrical Manufacturers Association LQ 1-77, General Purpose and Woodwork Institute of California Standards for Particleboard.

Low pressure laminated melamine: Melamine saturated sheets thermal-fused to a particleboard core. The material should meet the requirements of NEMA LQ 1-77, General Purpose.

Low pressure polyester overlay Cabinet Liner: Overlays comprised of polyester resin saturated cellulosic sheets thermo-bonded to the particleboard, hardboard, or plywood core. The resultant product has a solid color exposed surface which is durable and resistant to damage from abrasion and mild alkalies, acids and solvents, and meets the requirements of the following standards; National Electrical Manufacturers Association LQ 1-77, Light Duty and Woodwork Institute of California Standards for Particleboard.

Low pressure sodium lamp: A discharge lamp in which light is produced by radiation of sodium vapor at low pressure, producing a single wavelength of visible energy, i.e. yellow.

Low relief: See bas-relief.

Low rows: A quality defect sometimes found in woven carpet comprising rows of tufts having pile heights below specification. This condition occurs in Axminster weaving when the face yarn spools are almost empty.

Low voltage lamps: Incandescent lamps that operate at 6 to 12 volts.

Lozenge: A decorative motif in the shape of a diamond.

Lucite: A man made clear acrylic plastic.

Lumber: In the United States, in connection with building and manufacturing, wood as prepared for the market; whether in the log or in sawed or more elaborately dressed pieces. In Great Britain, such material is known simply as wood. As usually prepared for building purposes, lumber intended for the rougher operations of framing and the like is squared from the log in sawmills according to standard dimensions, but is otherwise undressed; while the lighter material, as for sheathing, ceiling, and other finish is commonly planed on one face and perhaps slightly molded, as with a tongue and groove, a bead, or the like. The British system of classifying wood under definite names, according to its dimensions, is quite unknown in the United States, except in a very general way. Thus, squared pieces for framing and the like are commonly all designated as Scantling when not more than about 30 square inches in cross section;

pieces of larger size being known as Timber, with or without the article. Thus, a piece 5"x 6" in size has been in the lumber trade more or less officially defined as a Scantling; a piece of 6" x 6" as a Dimension Timber. It is, therefore, in the United States, quite common to designate lumber by the use for which any given size may be primarily designed, as Studding, Furring, Sheathing, Veneer.

Lumen: The unit of luminous flux. It is the luminous flux emitted within a unit solid angle (one steradian) by a point source having a uniform luminous intensity of one candela.

Luminaire: A complete lighting unit consisting of a lamp or lamps together with the parts designed to distribute the light, to position and protect the lamps and to connect the lamps to the power supply.

Luminaire Dirt Depreciation: (LDD) The multiplier to be used in illuminance calculations to relate the initial illuminance provided by clean, new luminaries to the reduced illuminance that they will provide due to dirt collection on the luminaries at the time at which it is anticipated that cleaning procedures will be instituted.

Luminaire efficiency: The ratio of luminous flux (lumens) emitted by a luminaire to that emitted by the lamp or lamps used therein.

Luminance: The amount of light reflected or transmitted by an object.

Luster: (French) A crystal table light or wall sconce.

Luster: Brightness or reflectivity of fibers, yarns, carpets or fabrics. Synthetic fibers are produced in various luster classifications including bright, semi-bright, semi-dull, and dull. Bright fibers usually are clear (have no white pigment) whereas the duller designations have small amounts of white pigments such as titanium dioxide. Luster of finished carpet also depends upon yarn heat-setting methods, dyeing, and finishing. In high traffic commercial areas duller carpets are often preferred for soil hiding ability.

Lusterware: A silver, gold or platinum coating applied to ceramic ware to give it a lustrous shine.

Lux: The metric unit of illuminance. One lux is one lumen per square meter (lm/m^2).

Lyre-back chair: A chair in which the back is similar to a lyre and has metal strips to represent strings.

Lyre form: A wood furniture element that has the outline of a lyre, usually a chair.

M

Machined and knocked down: All pieces fully machined, ready for assembly.

Machined, smoothly: Free of defective manufacturing, with a minimum of 16 knife marks to the inch. Torn grain should not be permitted. Handling marks and/or grain raising due to moisture is not considered to be a defect.

Machine-printed wallpaper: Wallpaper that is printed on a press with rollers that have the design engraved on them.

Machine run: Not sanded after machining.

Magnolia: A hard wood pale in color used primarily in furniture making.

Mahogany: A hard wood red or brown in color and imported from Africa, Cuba and Brazil. It is expensive because it finishes well and is easy to work with.

Main support system: The frame or structural supporting system in a piece of furniture.

Maintenance Factor: (MF) A factor used in calculating illuminance after a given period of time and under given conditions. It takes into account temperature and voltage variations, dirt accumulation on luminaire and room surfaces, lamp depreciation, maintenance procedures and atmosphere conditions.

Majolica: Fourteenth century earthenware produced in Spain and Italy. It is glazed with tin and has painted designs.

Manchette: (French) A padded arm cushion.

Manifest: A document having the gross weight, consignor and consignee of a shipment.

Mantel: (A) A projecting hood or cover above a fireplace to collect the smoke and guide it into the chimney flue above (B) Same as Mantelpiece; a modern abbreviation.

Mantelpiece: Frame surrounding a fireplace. Often made of wood, stone or brick.

Manueline style: A Portuguese architectural style after King Manuel the Fortunate (1495-1521).

Manufactured building: A closed construction building assembly, or system of subassemblies, which may include structural, electrical, plumbing, heating, ventilating, or other service systems manufactured in manufacturing facilities for installation or erection, with or without other specified components, as a finished building or as part of a finished building, and may include residential, commercial, institutional, storage, and industrial structures.

Maple: A hard wood that is beige to reddish-brown in color and easy to work with.

Marble: Any stone consisting essentially of carbonate of lime, or the carbonates of lime and magnesia, and of such color and texture as to make it desirable for the higher grades of building, monumental, or decorative work. The varying shades of gray and the black colors of marbles are due to the presence of carbonaceous matter; the yellow, brown and red colors to iron oxides, and the green to the presence of silicate minerals, such as mica and talc. The veined and clouded effects are due to an unequal distribution of the coloring constituents throughout the mass of the stone.

Marbleizing: The art and practice of staining or coating a material, such as slate or cast iron, so as to resemble a surface of rich marble, the veins and cloudings being imitated by different expedients. Marbleized iron was formerly much used in the United States. This material was produced by a complete concealing of the surface, by a kind of paint in which the veins of marble were imitated. Recent work is done rather by staining the surface of inexpensive gray marble or slate, and some of the imitations are extremely truthful in appearance, and of decorative effect.

Markers: Colored yarns woven into the backs of woven carpets to aid installers in achieving correct pattern match and pile direction.

Marquetry: An inlaid piece of a material such as marble or wood, embedded into another to form a common design.

Marquise chair: The French version of a love seat. A seventeenth century chair that is very wide and has deep arms.

Marquise: (French) Small sofa.

Marquisette: Transparent fabric made of tightly twisted rayon, cotton, silk or nylon.

Martha Washington chair: A chair that has an upholstered seat, open arms and square or round tapered legs.

Mary Ann: The colloquial name for a method of stretching long lengths of carpet in commercial establishments by utilizing prepared wood planks when sufficient power stretchers are not available.

Masonry: The art and practice of building with stone,-natural or artificial,-with brick, and, by extension, with molded earth, as in adobe and pise; also, the work so produced. Stones and bricks are generally lain in mortar, but may be laid without it (dry masonry), care being taken so to superimpose the materials as to bind or bond together those below them.

Mastic: A heavy pliable adhesive used to seal joints.

Match: To bring to equality, uniformity, or similarity. Thus the planks of a floor are required to be matched in thickness, in width, as is customary in all floors of any elegance or finish, in color, also in surface, as for greater smoothness or a coarser or finer grain. By extension, and as applied to floor plank, sheathing, and the like, the term is held to include the working of tongues and grooves upon the edges; so that flooring spoken of as matched is understood to be tongued and grooved.

Match, set or drop: Pattern match designates the arrangement and dimensions of the repeating units comprising the design of patterned carpet, including woven patterns, prints, tufted high lows, and others. A typical pattern repeat might be 36" x 24". In set match, this rectangular pattern unit is arranged in parallel rows across the carpet width. In a half drop pattern, the start of each pattern repeat unit is transposed to the midpoint of the side of the adjacent unit. In the example, each adjacent unit starts 12 inches down the side of the neighboring one. In quarter drop match, each unit in the example would start six inches past the neighboring pattern unit's starting point. Thus, pattern repeat units in drop match repeat diagonally across the width, and in set match they repeat straight across the width perpendicularly to the length. Pattern repeat dimensions and match are significant to specifiers and purchasing agents because they influence the amount of excess carpet (over measured area) needed in multiple width installations.

Matelasse: Fabric with quilt-like raised patterns.

Material: Any of several different kinds of building supplies such as timber, concrete and insulation.

Material only: Run to pattern only. Not assembled, nor machined for assembly, nor cut to length. The terms loose and long and mill run mean the same as material only.

Matte surface: A nonglossy dull surface, as opposed to a shiny (specular) surface. Light reflected from a matter surface is diffuse.

Matting: Severe pile crush combined with entanglement of fibers and tufts.

Media room: A room that has sound and screening equipment, and television all in one room.

Mediterranean style: A twentieth century style that has heavy carvings and scales and uses wrought iron or leather as trim.

Medium density fiberboard: A dry formed panel product manufactured from lignocellulosic fibers combined with a synthetic resin or other suitable binder. The panels are compressed to a density of 31 pounds per cubic foot to 50 pounds per cubic foot in a hot press by a process in which substantially the entire inter-fiber bond is created by the added binder. Other materials may have been added during manufacture to improve certain properties. The product should meet the standards of National Particleboard Association NPA 4-73.

Member: An individual piece of solid stock or plywood which forms an item of millwork.

Menagere: (French) A dresser with open shelves for a bowl and pitcher.

Mercury lamp: A high intensity discharge (HID) lamp in which the major portion of the light is produced by radiation from mercury. Includes clear, phosphor-coated and self-ballasted lamps.

Meridienne: (French) A sofa with one arm higher than the other. A daybed that is short and has a sloped top.

Metal halide lamp: A high intensity discharge (HID) lamp in which the major portion of the light is produced by radiation from mercury. Includes clear, phosphor-coated and self-ballasted lamps.

Metal work: (A) Work done by melting metal and molding or casting it in forms which can then be more or less finished by hand, as with cutting tools and files. (B) Work done by hammering and beating into shape metal either hot or cold. The decoration of metal by means of inlay of different kinds is reducible to one of the two systems above named, except where it is a result of engraving, as in damascened work; but such ornamentation as this hardly enters into architectural practice of any period. The soldering of small parts together is common in jewelery, but only in rare cases in connection with building. The use of wire concerns only lathing and such simple railing as is used temporarily or in slight structures. Engraving upon metal is used in what is known as the Memorial Brass, and the engraved lines were filled with some colored material. Enamelling is used upon tombs, but chiefly in details of heraldry or of the costume of portrait statues.

Metallic fiber: Synthetic fiber made of metal, metal coated plastic, or plastic coated metal sometimes used in small amounts in carpet to dissipate static electricity, thus preventing shock.

Mezzanine: A small floor that is between two main floors.

Mil: A unit of length equal to 0.001 inch. Often used for specifying the thickness and/or width of filaments, ribbons, films and foils.

Milk glass: A glass that is white and clear.

Millefiori: Different colored pieces of glass fused together then cut crosswise, joined and embedded in clear glass and then blown into the desired shape.

Mill end: A shot piece of carpet roll goods having a length less than that of a full shipping roll or short roll but greater than a remnant. Quality standards differ among mills, but a mill end length specification of nine to 20 feet is typical.

Mill run: Run to pattern only, Not assembled, nor machined for assembly, nor cut to length. The terms "material only" and "loose and long" mean the same as "mill run."

Millwork: Architectural woodwork and related items.

Miniature: A painting that is 10"-14" high.

Minton porcelain: Earthenware decorated in the Chinese style and first produced in 1793.

Miroir: (French) Mirror.

Mirror: A surface, made of silvered glass, obsidian, silver, gold and metal that reflects images almost perfectly.

Mission furniture: A style of furniture started by the Spanish missionaries in California dominated by crude furniture upholstered with leather and copper nails for trim.

Miter: The joining of two members at an angle that bisects the angle of junction.

Miter, lock: A miter joint employing a tongue and groove working to further strengthen the joint.

Miter, shoulder: Any type of a miter joint that presents a shoulder, such as a lock miter or a splined miter.

Mobile: A sculpture that will move with the natural current of the air. Usually made for decoration.

Modacrylic fibers: See Acrylics.

Modesty panel: The panel set on the back of a kneehole desk to maintain privacy.

Modular furniture: Furniture pieces that can be arranged in any way according to the style of the designers.

Module: A flexible unit of measure valued for prefabricated building components. The basic measurement usually is four inches.

Mohair: Fabric woven from Angora goat wool.

Moire: A wavy surface effect in a fabric caused by a special weaving technique.

Moisture content: The weight of the water in the wood expressed in percentage of the weight of the oven-dry wood.

Mold: (A) A form used to guide a workman, whether a solid object requiring to be exactly copied or reproduced by casting, or a profile cut out of a board or piece of sheet metal. In the second of these characters the mold is used for running plaster moldings and the like. (B) The hollow into which melted metal, liquid plaster, or the like is poured in the process of casting. Such a mold is itself a direct case or impression of a mold in sense A. (C) Same as molding; a common abbreviation used by the trades in composition, as bed mold.

Molding: A wooden or plastic strip attached to the bottom of a baseboard or wall to cover the joint between wall and floor. Ornamental shapes used on tables, frames or ceilings.

Moldings: Contours given to trimmings and projections.

Monofilament: A yarn composed of a single continuous strand of synthetic polymer.

Moresque: A multicolor carpet made from moresque yarns.

Moresque yarns are produced by plytwisting two or more single yarns of different colors or shades. Moresque yarns thus have a barber pole appearance. Moresque carpets in suitable colors are good soil hiders in high traffic areas.

Morocco: A type of leather that comes from goat skin.

Mortice and tenon joint: A joint formed by a projecting piece fitting or tenon into a socket or mortice.

Mosaic: Surface decoration or design made up of small pieces of glass, marble or stone.

Mother-of-pearl: The inner section of pearl oysters or abalone shells that have a pretty luster.

Motif: The main or dominant design or idea used in a work of art, furniture or architecture.

Mouchette: A curved motif in tracery in the form of a dagger.

Muffin stand: A table that is used to hold a tea service and plates.

Mullion: A slender, vertical, intermediate member forming part of a framework, or serving to subdivide an opening or the like. The term is, perhaps, to be considered as referring to an accessory piece introduced for ornament or for some subordinate purpose, rather than to a supporting member forming part of the general construction. The strips of wood or another material that divide a window into two or more sections.

Multifilament: Synthetic yarns composed of a multiplicity of continuous fibrous strands extruded together, usually from the multiple holes of a single spinneret. Multifilament carpet yarns are texturized to increase bulk and cover, and are called bulked continuous filament yarns or simply BCF yarns.

Muntin: A small, slender mullion in light framing, as a sash bar, a middle stile of a door. The vertical part in a door or window frame which butts into the horizontal rails. A sash bar.

Mural: A picture painted onto a wall and often a public wall.

Mushrabeyeh work: Wooden lattices used to cover upper windows in Islamic houses.

Muslin: Plain medium-weight cotton cloth. Often used unbleached.

N

Nail: A slender and small piece of material, usually metal, intended to be driven into anything, especially a board, plank, joist, or other wooden member, for the purpose of holding fast, usually by the elastic force of the wood pressing against it. The term is usually confined to the above described form, but in composition (as in Treenail or Trenail) a different signification is implied, which does not generally concern the architect or builder.

Nail, cut: One cut by a machine, as distinguished from wrought and wire nails. The invention of the cut nail machine, together with the increase of woodworking machinery, producing cheap clapboards, shingles, etc., was largely instrumental in developing the wooden building of the United States. The metal of the cut nail is compressed by the machine so much that it is too brittle to be clinched; but it is practicable to soften it sufficiently by heating and allowing it to cool slowly.

Nap: The pile yarns or the surface of a rug or carpet.

Napping shears: Hand shears designed by the manufacturer to trim pile tufts protruding on the surface of the carpet level with the surrounding tufts.

Narrow carpet: Woven carpet 27 or 36 inches wide.

Narrow width carpet: A carpet manufactured in widths less than nine feet.

Natural gray yarn: Unbleached and undyed yarn spun from a blend of black, brown, or gray wools.

Needle: (A) Tufting-An eyed needle which inserts yarns into primary backing to form tufts. (B) Needlepunching-Barbed felting needles which entangle and compress fibrous fleeces into needled felts such as those used for outdoor carpet. (C) Knitting-Hooked needles that form the loops of knitted fabric.

Needle bar: Tufting machine part that holds the needles and carries them up and down. Also, that part of a knitting machine on which needles are mounted.

Needle board: Part of a needle loom or fiber locker in which a multiplicity of downward pointing barbed felting needles are mounted.

It is attached to a beam that moves up and down. On the down stroke, felting needles penetrate a fiber batt or fleece, compressing it into a felted fabric.

Needle Loom: A machine for producing needled felt fabrics, also called needle-punched fabrics, which are sometimes used as outdoor carpet. The needle loom converts fiber directly to fabric by entangling and compressing fleece with barbed felting needles. (Note: Needle Loom also denotes certain narrow weaving looms used in tape production having a needle instead of a shuttle as the fill insertion device. These have no application to carpet.)

Needlepoint: Wool threads embroidered in a diagonal design.

Needlepunched carpets: This fabric is fabricated by first laying down many strands of the carpet fiber in a loose random fashion. More of the fibers are strewn on top until the accumulated layers of fiber reach a predetermined height. Next, a solid sheet of polypropylene is placed over this blanket of fibers and more layers of the fiber are placed on top of the sheet. Then the needle bonding machine punches literally thousands of needles through these layers of loosely placed carpet fibers at the top and bottom with the solid sheet in between. This punching action of the machine compressed the sandwich into a solid mass, interlocking and bonding the fibers to themselves as well as to the middle sheet. Additional layers of carpet fibers are then applied and the fabric is needlepunched again. The number of layers and needlepunching steps are governed by the desired thickness of the completed carpet. Needlepunched carpets were first made of polypropylene fibers in solid colors for use as outdoor carpets on patios, terraces, porches, around swimming pools, etc. As such, they provided excellent wear and color fastness. Now they are made for indoor use as well as for outdoors and are popularly called Indoor-Outdoor carpet. For indoor use they are made of wool, nylon, acrylic or olefin fibers. No longer limited to solid colors, they are also available in several colors printed in a wide variety of designs. New manufacturing techniques now produce actual pile effects as well as the original flat surface. Some grades of needlepunched carpet are fabricated with a sponge rubber or other backing material

Needle-punching: A method for manufacturing felt fabrics in which fiber batts or fleeces are compressed by the entangling action of barbed needles. Needlepunched carpet made from solution-dyed polypropylene is often used as outdoor carpet. Needlepunched nylon carpet is often printed and foam backed for indoor use.

Needlepunched carpets: This fabric is fabricated by first laying down many strands of the carpet fiber in a loose random fashion. More of the fibers are strewn on top until the accumulated layers of fiber reach a predetermined height. Next, a solid sheet of polypropylene is placed over this blanket of fibers and more layers of the fiber are placed on top of the sheet. Then the needle bonding machine punches literally thousands of needles through these layers of loosely placed carpet fibers at the top and bottom with the solid sheet in between. This punching action of the machine compressed the sandwich into a solid mass, interlocking and bonding the fibers to themselves as well as to the middle sheet. Additional layers of carpet fibers are then applied and the fabric is needlepunched again. The number of layers and needlepunching steps are governed by the desired thickness of the completed carpet. Needlepunched carpets were first made of polypropylene fibers in solid colors for use as outdoor carpets on patios, terraces, porches, around swimming pools, etc. As such, they provided excellent wear and color fastness. Now they are made for indoor use as well as for outdoors and are popularly called Indoor-Outdoor carpet. For indoor use they are made of wool, nylon, acrylic or olefin fibers. No longer limited to solid colors, they are also available in several colors printed in a wide variety of designs. New manufacturing techniques now produce actual pile effects as well as the original flat surface. Some grades of needlepunched carpet are fabricated with a sponge rubber or other backing material

Needle-punching: A method for manufacturing felt fabrics in which fiber batts or fleeces are compressed by the entangling action of barbed needles. Needlepunched carpet made from solution-dyed polypropylene is often used as outdoor carpet. Needlepunched nylon carpet is often printed and foam backed for indoor use.

Nest of tables: A set of tables in which each table is smaller than the next enabling them to fit under each other.

Newel: A post located at the bottom of a flight of stairs that supports the railing.

Ninon: Sheer plain-weave drapery fabric of nylon, silk or rayon.

Noil: Short fiber removed during combing of wool or other natural fiber, particularly during worsted yarn production. It may subsequently be separately spun into yarn using the woolen system or other method capable of handling short fiber.

Nonbearing wall: A nonstructural wall or partition.

Nonglare glass: A glass used in picture frames that is nonreflecting.

Nonwoven: Any fabric manufactured by a method other than weaving but particularly those fabrics composed of fibers held together by chemical, mechanical, adhesive or fusion means. In popular usage knitted fabrics are not considered to be nonwovens.

Nosing: The front dividing line of a step, where the top of a riser joins the front of a tread. The front edge of the tread that projects beyond the riser immediately below the tread.

Nottingham earthenware: A thirteenth century pottery that is brown and has a light metallic luster. The last authentic piece was made in 1799.

Noyer: (French) Walnut.

Nylon: Nylon, the first of the truly synthetic fibers, was engineered for carpet use in the 1940's and it has since become synonymous with strength and abrasion resistance. Its characteristics are good resilience, outstanding resistance to abrasion, good texture retention, and good cleanability. Some are specially engineered to possess excellent soil hiding as well as anti-static properties. Synthetic thermoplastic of the polyamide family. It may be melt extruded into filaments useful for carpet yarn. Nylon is by far the dominant fiber in tufted carpet pile yarns. Two chemical types, nylon-6,6 and nylon-6, are used in carpet. Nylon-6,6 is poly (hexamethyleneadipamide) and nylon-6 is polycaprolactam.

O

Oak: A hard wood that is pale yellow-brown in color and mainly used for furniture because of its durability.

Objet d'art: (French) Any small art object.

Obscure glass: Glass that is translucent.

Occasional table: A table that can be used easily at any time.

Offices: Buildings used only for professional use and are not used for any living purposes.

Ogee molding: A double curved molding. It is concave above and convex below.

Oily yarn: Yarn containing excessive oil on its surface, usually from too much oiling of rings on spinning and twisting machines. Although not visible during carpet production, it may appear soiled or as dark lines of yarn when the carpet is in service. The problem is insignificant in piece-dyed carpet which is washed during the dye cycle, but appears in carpet made from stock-dyed yarn which is not subjected to wet processing after weaving of tufting.

Olefin (polypropylene): This carpet fiber was produced as still another synthetic fiber a few years after the acrylics came on the scene, about 1965. A solution dyed version of the fiber is used in indoor-outdoor carpets. In addition, a considerable amount of this fiber is used in backing materials. The characteristics of olefin fibers are good resistance to abrasion, good soil resistance and cleanability, adequate resilience and texture retention, particularly when used in a tight constructed fabric. Any long chain synthetic polymer composed of at least 85% by weight of ethylene, propylene or other olefin units. Polypropylene yarns are used in carpets.

Opaque finish: A paint or pigmented stain finish that hides the natural characteristics and color of the grain of the wood surface and is not transparent.

Open step: A step with a tread that does not end at one or both sides at a wall.

Organdy: Plain-weave, tightly spun cotton cloth.

Oriental Rugs: Handwoven rugs made in the Middle East and the Orient.

Ormoulu: (French) (A) Gilded bronze. (B) An alloy used to decorate furniture and consisting of copper and tin or zinc which resembles gold.

Orthographic projection: The projection of perpendicular lines to the plane of projection.

Ottoman: A cushioned stool with no legs visible.

Outdoor carpet: Carpet which may be used outdoors without rapid fading or deterioration. The principal requirements are resistance to sunlight and water. Most outdoor carpet pile yarns are solution dyed polypropylene containing ultraviolet stabilization additives. Coatings and backing materials are synthetics that are water and rot resistant.

Outbond: Bonded, or forming a bond, along the face of a wall, as in the case of stretchers. Composed largely or entirely of stretchers.

Outlet box: A box connecting the electrical outlet to the conduit.

Overdoor: A decoration over the door and on the wall such as, carvings or a bas-relief.

Oxbow front: The carved section of an eighteenth century chest.

P

P'ai Lou: An ornamental Chinese arch.

Package dyeing: A dyeing process in which finished pile yarns are first wound onto large perforated forms. Then heated dyes are forced through the perforations onto the yarns. The yarns are dried, unwound and then tufted or woven without further processing.

Padding: A cushioning material made of felted cattle hair and jute, or rubber, or plastic foam, or other resilient materials used as an underlayment of rugs and carpets. Also known in the industry as cushion or underlay.

Pad foot: The part of a cabriole leg which is flat.

Paint: A liquid solution that has a pigment mixed into another solution such as water, oil, or an organic solvent.

Paisley: A cotton, silk or wool fabric with swirled woven or printed shapes. An Indian shawl. A design having curved shapes that are derived from the palmette shape.

Palisander: A French term for Brazilian rosewood. It is a hard wood flesh pink to purplish in color.

Palmette: A fan-shaped ornament derived from palm leaves.

Panelboard: Circuit breakers, fuses, and switches mounted on an insulated panel.

Paneling: Wooden boards used to cover a wall or ceiling.

Panetiere: (French) Bread box. A bread box designed with leaves and flowers which usually sits on a table.

Panier: (French) Basket.

Parabolic louvers: A grid of baffles which redirect light downward and provide very low luminaire brightness.

Parallel edge: A drafting tool, such as *Mayline* or *Paradraft*, which is mounted with cable on the drawing board. It moves smoothly up and down, remaining parallel, but without the hand tension required of the T-square. This is much preferred over the T-square for serious drafters. The kind purchased separately and mounted on top of the board is much smoother than the type that comes integrated with the board by the factory. It is simple to install.

Pardon screen: A screen surrounding or placed before a confessional, to hide the penitent from public view during the act of confession.

PAR lamps: Parabolic aluminized reflector lamps which offer excellent beam control, come in a variety of beam patterns from very narrow spot to wide flood, and can be used outdoors unprotected because they are made of hard glass that can withstand adverse weather.

Parlor: The primary room for entertaining guests and, until the twentieth century, considered a living room.

Parquet: Thin hardwood flooring laid in patterns. It is often inlaid and highly polished.

Parquetry: An inlay pattern of geometrical designs usually done with several colors and with stone or wood.

Particleboard: A mat-formed flat panel consisting of particles of wood bonded together with a synthetic resin or other suitable binder. The particles are classified by size and dried to a uniform moisture content,

after which they are mixed with a binder, mat-formed into a panel, compressed to proper density and then cured under heat and pressure. In millwork construction, whether as particleboard alone or as core material for plywood, the particleboard should meet the requirements of ANSI A208.1-79 Table I Grade 1-M-3. However, when used for core materials for flush veneered doors in Section 20, it should meet the requirements of ANSI A208.1-79 Table I Grade 1-l-1.

Partners' desk: An eighteenth century desk that allows two people to sit opposite one another.

Party wall: A wall that is shared between two buildings.

Pastiche: A satirical design based on another designer's style and manner.

Patch: A repair made by inserting and securely gluing a sound piece of wood of the same species in a place of a defect that has been removed. The edges shall be cut clean and sharp and fit tight with no voids. Boat patches are oval shaped with sides tapering in each direction to a point or to a small rounded end; router patches have parallel sides and rounded ends; sled patches are rectangular with feathered ends.

Patchwork: A design or piece of cloth made of small pieces of fabric sewn together.

Patera: A flat, oval or circular ornament often decorated with acanthus leaves. Common in classical architecture.

Patina: The result of oxidation in copper and copper alloys. It can also refer to the sheen furniture develops with age.

Patio: An inner courtyard open to the sky. An outdoor seating area attached to a house, often covered. Common in North and Latin American architecture.

Pattern: Artistic decorative design on the surface of carpet. It may be printed, woven with colored yarns, or sculptured in multiple pile heights.

Pattern control: A blade, in the air passage of an air handling luminaire, which sets the direction of air flow from the luminaire.

Pattern streaks: Visually apparent streaking in patterned carpet resulting from linear juxtaposition of pattern elements in one direction. It is usually most visible in the length direction. It is not a carpet defect, but is inherent in certain designs.

Contract specifiers should view rolls of carpet laid out on a floor to evaluate geometric or other busy patterns for this characteristic which may be objectionable in long corridors and other large areas but not visible in small rooms.

Peacock chair: An armchair made from rattan with a high back.

Pedestal: (A) A support consisting of a base, dado and a cornice used for tables. (B) The base supporting a column or colonnade or for a piece of sculpture or objet d'art. (C) The drawer unit supporting or suspended from the top of a desk.

Pediment: A low-pitched gable above a portico.

Pelmet: The frame found on three sides of a window usually covered with fabric.

Pembroke table: A table with drop leaves supported by brackets.

Pencil pointer: A drafting tool to sharpen the point of drafting lead. The basic type with steel cutter is recommended over other types. It has several bushings for different pencil diameters, and has a gauge for blunt or sharp cutting. A sand-paper board is good for rendering and sketching. It can chisel and blunt leads for special techniques.

Pendant: A boss elongated so that it hangs down.

Pennsylvania Dutch furniture: Eighteenth century furniture made from walnut, maple or pine and decorated with animals, hearts, flowers or fruits.

Penthouse: The top floor of an office or residential building, usually a living space. A subsidiary structure on top of another structure with a lean-to or other separate roof.

Percale: Lightweight woven cotton cloth.

Petite-commode: (French) A small table with three drawers.

Petit point: Small stitched needlepoint done on canvas.

Pew: A wooden church bench or seat.

Pewter: An alloy combination of lead and tin, antimony or copper.

Phenolics: Plastics that can withstand heat up to 330 degrees F and are very strong. They are resistant to fire, acids, and oils. Phenolics are poor heat conductors and will yellow due to light exposure. It is mainly used for appliance parts, handles for utensils and electrical insulation.

Philadelphia Chippendale: Eighteenth century furniture noted for its likeness to Chippendale furniture.

Pickled finish: The white finish that appears when old paint is removed.

Picks per inch: In woven carpet and fabric the number of fill yarns per inch of length.

Picture plane: (PP) The two-dimension plane that the observer sees through. It is perpendicular to the observer's sight line and all lines from the observer to the object cross through it.

Piece dyed: Carpet dyed by immersion into an aqueous dye bath.

Piecrust table: An eighteenth century table with scalloped edges.

Pier table: A table that stands against a wall between two doors or windows.

Pierced work: Decoration which consists mainly or partially of perforations. The essential character of this kind of perforations are intended to be seen as accentuated points of light against dark or dark against light.

Pigment: Highly colored insoluble powdered substance used to impart color to other materials. White pigments, e.g., titanium dioxide, are dispersed in fiber forming polymers to produce delustered (semidull and dull) fibers.

Pigmented yarns: Same as solution dyed or dope dyed yarns.

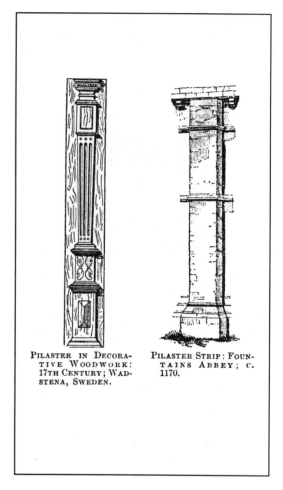

PILASTER IN DECORA-
TIVE WOODWORK:
17TH CENTURY; WAD-
STENA, SWEDEN.

PILASTER STRIP: FOUN-
TAINS ABBEY; C.
1170.

Pilaster: A shallow pier projecting from a wall. A column or pier with a capitol and a base.

Pile: The visible wear surface of carpet, consisting of yarn tufts in loop and/or cut configuration. Sometimes called the face or nap.

Pile crush: Loss of pile thickness by compression and bending of tufts caused by traffic and heavy furniture. The tufts collapse into the air space between them. It may be irreversible if the yarn has inadequate resilience and/or the pile has insufficient density for the traffic load.

Pile density: See Density.

Pile height: The height of the pile, as measured in decimal parts of one inch, from the top surface of the back to the top surface of the pile. The higher the number, the higher the pile. The length of the extended tufts measured from the primary backing top surface to their tips. Pile tufts should be gently extended but not stretched during this measurement. This specification is usually expressed in fractions or decimal fractions of an inch in the U.S. and sometimes in millimeters elsewhere.

Pile setting: Carpet cleaners' term for the process of erecting the damp and disheveled pile after shampooing by means of a pile brush or pile lifting machine.

Pile weight: The weight of the pile yarns as expressed in ounces per square yard. The more ounces per square yard of surface yarns the denser the pile.

Pile wire: Part of a carpet weaving loom consisting of a metal strip or rod on which the pile tufts are formed.

Pile yarn: The yarn which forms the tufts of the carpet. Also called Face Yarn.

Pillar: A free-standing member of any shape as opposed to a column which conforms to a classical shape.

Pilling: A condition of the carpet face (which may occur from heavy traffic) in which fibers from different tufts become entangled with one another forming hard masses of fibers and tangled tufts. Pills may be cut off with scissors.

Pills: The tiny round pieces of fiber that gathers on the surface of fabric due to abrasion.

Pill test: Carpet flammability test described in federal regulations CPSC 1-70 and CPSC 2-70. It measures flammability as a function of the size of burn produced by timed burning tablet (Methenamine). Also used on the back of carpet. All carpet sold in the United States must pass the CPSC 1-70 flammability test.

Pine: A soft wood, white or pale yellow in color which can either be clear or knotty.

Pineapple: An ornamental motif used as a finial on bedposts and other furniture. Commonly used in England and in the Southern U.S. as a finial on decorative entrance door heads to indicate welcome.

Piping: Material encased in a cord used for binding the edge of upholstered furniture.

Pitch: (A) An accumulation of resin which occurs in separations in the wood or in the wood cells

themselves. (B) Indicates the closeness of the pile tufts along the width of a woven carpet as expressed in the number of warp or lengthwise lines contained in every 27 inches of width. The higher the pitch number, such as 180, 189, 216, etc., then the closer the pile tufts are to each other widthwise in the carpet. See Gauge. (C) The physical response given to frequency. (D) The slanting incline of a roof or horizontal pipe.

Pitch pocket: A well defined opening between the annual growth rings, which contains pitch. (A) A very small pocket is a maximum of 1/16" x 3" in length, or 1/8" x 2" in length. (B) A small pocket is a maximum of 1/16" x 6" in length, or 1/8" x 4" in length. (C) A medium pocket is a maximum of 1/16" x 12", or 1/8" x 8".

Pitch streak: A well defined accumulation of pitch in the wood cells in a more or less regular streak. (A) A very small pitch streak is a maximum of 1/16" x 12", or 1/8" x 6". (B) A small streak is a maximum of 1/8" x 12", or 1/4" x 6". (C) A medium streak is a maximum of 1/4" x 16", or 3/8" x 12".

Placage: (French) Veneering.

Plan: The horizontal design or arrangement of building parts as well as the drawing that represents it.

Plaque: Flat, thin pieces of wood, metal, porcelain, etc. used for wall ornamentation.

Plaster of Paris: A mixture made from gypsum and heated in a kiln which hardens when mixed with water.

Plastic: A substance made from polymerized organic compounds which can be shaped into products.

Plastic backing sheet: A thin sheet, usually phenolic, applied under pressure to the back of a laminated plastic panel to achieve balance by equalizing the rate of moisture absorption or emission.

Plate rail: A grooved horizontal decorative wall molding used to display plates.

Plied yarn: A yarn composed of two or more single yarns twisted together. Many 2-ply yarns are used in carpet. In cut-pile carpet (e.g. Saxony) plied yarns must be heat-set to prevent untwisting under traffic. Multiple continuous filament yarns made by fiber producers are

sometimes air-entangled rather than twisted together.

Plinth: The base of a column or doorway; also a support for sculpture.

Plisse: Puckered cotton or synthetic fabric made by treating the fibers with caustic soda.

Plow: A rectangular groove or slot of three surfaces cut parallel with the grain of a wood member, in contrast to a dado, which is cut across the grain.

Plug-in Wiring: Electrical distribution system which has quick-connect wiring connectors.

Plush: Cut-pile closely woven fabric made from cotton, silk, rayon, etc.

Plush Finish: A smooth carpet surface texture in which individual tufts are only minimally visible and the overall visual effect is that of a single level of fiber ends. This finish is normally achieved only on cut-pile carpet produced from nonheat-set single spun yarns by brushing and shearing.

Ply: A single end component in a plied yarn, or the number which tells how many single ends have been ply-twisted together to form a plied yarn, e.g., 2-ply or 3-ply. A thickness of carpet yarn. 3-ply means that each tuft of yarn consists of 3 yarns spun together to form the tuft.

Plywood: A panel composed of a crossbanded assembly of layers or plies of veneer, or veneers in combination with a lumber core or particleboard core, that are joined with an adhesive. Except for special constructions, the grain of alternate plies is always approximately at right angles, and the thickness and species on either side of the core are identical for balanced effect. An odd number of plies is always used.

Point method lighting calculation: A lighting design procedure for predetermining the illuminance at various locations in lighting installations, by use of luminaire photometric data.

Polarization: The process by which the transverse vibrations of light waves are oriented in a specific plane. Polarization may be obtained by using either transmitting or reflecting media.

Pole screen: See fire screen.

Polychrome: Characterized by many different colors.

Polyester: A fiber-forming thermoplastic synthetic polymer used in some carpet fiber. Essentially all polyester carpet fiber is staple and the yarns are spun yarns. Polyester for carpet is made from terephthalic acid and ethylene glycol and is known chemically as poly (ethylene terephthalate). Polyester fibers were introduced still later and became increasingly popular because of their soft, luxurious appearance close to that of wool as well as their bright lustrous shades. They possess a good resistance to abrasion, very good resilience and texture retention, and adequate cleanability.

Polyethylene: A chemical and stain resistant plastic. It is often used for toys, ice cube trays and dishes. Polyethylene is flexible and can withstand heat up to 100 degrees Fahrenheit.

Polymers: High molecular weight chemical compounds formed by repeated linking of smaller chemical units called monomers. Polymers from which fibers are made are long chain molecules in which the monomers are linked end to end linearly. Synthetic polymers used for carpet fiber include nylon-6, 6 and nylon-6 (polyamides), polyester, polypropylene, and polyacrylonitrile (acrylics). In popular terminology, polymers are also called plastics or resins.

Polyester decorative paper edging: A two or more ply cured polyester saturated decorative paper a minimum of 12 mils in thickness. A high viscosity hot-melt adhesive may be pre-applied to the edging. The edging shall be applied to the panel with 375° to 450° heat and pressure. The surface shall withstand 500° temperature without blistering. The surface shall meet the requirements of NEMA LD 3-80. The adhesive, whether pre-applied or not, shall be a pigment extended, resin modified, ethylene-vinyl acetate co-polymer base, hot-melted adhesive. Physical properties of this glue are as follows. (A) Viscosity at 200° 75M - 100 CPS (B) Ring and Ball melting point 97°-101° C (C) Penetrameter, 150 grs. at 25° C 6.0-8.0.

Polypropylene: A plastic that resists abrasion and is very hard. It is used for electrical insulation and can be laminated by cloth, paper and aluminum. Synthetic thermoplastic polymer used for molded items, sheets, films, and fibers. FTC (U.S. government) classification is Olefin. The polymer is made by stereospecific polymerization of propylene. Most polypropylene carpet fiber is solution dyed and sometimes contains ultraviolet stabilizers for outdoor use. Printable modifications are available but not extensively used. The carpet fiber is available as both bulked continuous filament yarns and staple for spun yarn production.

Polyvinyl edging: Application: Vinyl (PVC) Edging on seamless rolls to be applied on single/double side edge banding machines using hot-melt adhesives. Specifications; Product to be calendered, of wood design, grained or smooth material, solid color. Product to be chip proof, flame resistant and impervious to moisture. Thickness of 0.45 mm (0.0177"), 0.40 mm (0.0157"), 0.60 mm (0.0256") with tolerance of $\pm$ 0.001" and tear strength of approximately 1800 lbs. per sq. in. Product to be antistatic and equipped with an adhesive agent for bonding.

Pontil mark: The mark that occurs from an iron rod used in working molten glass.

Poppyhead: An ornamental termination or finial of a bench carved with foliage or figures.

Porcelain: Ceramic ware that is hard and translucent and was discovered in China about 800 A. D.

Porosity test: A method of determining the degree of porosity of a concrete floor before attempting to install carpeting by the glue down method. It is usually done by pouring a cupful of water in several scattered areas and observing the results. If the water is absorbed it indicates the floor is porous. If the water remains on the surface or breaks up into beads, it denotes the floor is relatively nonabsorbant.

Porringer: A bowl used for hot wine drinks made from pewter or silver.

Porte-cochere: A covered driveway associated with an office building, hotel, etc.

Portico: A porch supported by columns. A roofed space forming the entrance of a building.

Pottery: Any kind of dish made from clay and fired in a kiln, such as ceramics, earthenware and stoneware.

Poudreuse: (French) Powder or toilet table. An eighteenth century dressing table with a folding top and a mirror on the under side.

Pouf: An ottoman that is upholstered and round and popular in the nineteenth century.

Powder: A carpet cleaning preparation consisting of absorbent granules impregnated with dry cleaning fluids, detergents, and other cleaners. The dry powder is sprinkled on the carpet, worked into the pile with a brush, left to absorb soil for a short time, and finally removed with the absorbed soil by vacuuming.

Powered pile brush: In addition to its vacuuming capability, it contains a self-contained mechanically driven brush cylinder which provides a rigorous agitation to the carpet surface to open and erect the pile. It is used as well to supplement the periodic shampooing of most carpet constructions.

Power stretcher: An installation tool used to stretch longer areas of carpet than can properly be done by the knee kicker. The back end is braced against an immovable object such as a wall, post, etc. Extended tubes are added on for the approximate distance of desired stretch. Then the head, containing rows of angle sharp steel pins adjustable in length to extend into the pile and a short distance into the carpet backing is connected. The down movement of the handle attached to the head causes the head and the carpet to move forward several inches and thus stretch the carpet from the back end of the tool to the head.

Precast concrete: Factory manufactured concrete components.

Prefabrication: Manufacturing of building components prior to assembly into a building.

Preheat fluorescent lamp: A fluorescent lamp designed for operation in a circuit requiring a manual or automatic starting switch to preheat the electrodes in order to start the arc.

Preservative: A treating solution which prevents decay in wood; having the ability to preserve wood by inhibiting the growth of decay fungi.

Pressed glass: A type of glass pressed in a mold developed in 1825 in the United States.

Prie-dieu: A seventeenth century stand with a kneeling ledge used for prayer.

Pretrimmed wallpaper: Wallpaper that has a selvage.

Primary backing: A component of tufted carpet consisting of woven or nonwoven fabric into which pile yarn tufts are inserted by the tufting needles. It is the carrier fabric for the pile yarn and should not be confused with secondary backing which is a reinforcing fabric laminated to the back of tufted carpet subsequent to the tufting process. Most primary backing is either woven or nonwoven polypropylene, although woven jute is still sometimes used. Some synthetic primary backings have nylon fiber attached to their upper surfaces to make them union dyeable with nylon pile yarns.

Primavera: A hard wood light in color with a stripe in the grain.

Prime coat: The coat of paint that is first and seals the pores in the surface.

Prime urethane cushion: Separate carpet underpad made from virgin polyurethane foam. The sheet of foam is cut from large loaves. As opposed to prime cushion, rebonded polyurethane is made from recovered scrap.

Prince of Wales plumes: A decoration made of three ostrich feathers tied together and used on furniture.

Print: A design that is transferred from another medium.

Printed Carpet: (A) Carpet having colored patterns applied by methods analogous to those used for printing flat textiles and paper. These include flatbed screen printing employing woven fabric screens, rotary screen printing with perforated sheet steel screens, Stalwart printing employing sponge rubber pattern elements on wooden rollers, and modern computer programmed jet printing. (B) As the name implies, colored designs of all varieties are printed directly on the pile of constructed carpet. The carpet is first manufactured with uncolored pile and then the pattern is applied to the yarns. Generally, one of two printing techniques are used. One process uses embossed cylinders to imprint the designs. Several of these cylinders are used in tandem, each printing a different color, to produce colorful and sometimes intricate designs on the face of the carpet. The second process is screen printing. The dye is forced through flat templates or flat bed and roller screens to produce the finished designs on the pile of the carpet. Each color requires the use of a separate screen.

Production furniture: Furniture which is manufactured or reupholstered for sale rather than custom made to order.

Profile: A molding section or contour. The outline of an object or building.

Psyche: (French) Cheval glass.

Puckering: An installation defect in carpet seams in which one side is longer than the adjoining carpet edge. The excess carpet gathers into wrinkles or pleats at the seam.

Pull-up chair: A chair without arms.

Purchase order: An order form giving details of a purchase.

Purple heart: See amaranth.

Q

Quadratura: Trompe l'oeil painting as wall decoration.

Quadriga: A sculpture group composed of a four horse chariot. Used as a monument or the crown of a facade.

Quarter: A woven carpet term that designates the width of narrow carpet. It is one quarter of a yard, or nine inches. At one time most woven carpet was made on narrow looms. Widths such as 27 inches and 36 inches were commonly called three-quarter and four-quarter carpet, respectively.

Quarter round: Molding that is shaped into a quarter circle.

Quatrefoil: A decoration on Gothic furniture consisting of four flowers, petals, or leaves.

Queen's ware: Earthenware developed in 1762 by Josiah Wedgewood.

Quilt: A covering for a bed made with two layers and stuffed in the middle. Often several different fabrics will be used, and pieced together in patterns forming the top, then stitched through the padding to the bottom, producing the characteristic high-low or quilted effect.

R

Rabbet: A continuous small recess, generally understood as having a right angle included between its sides, especially one whose sides enclose a relatively restricted area; one formed by two planes very narrow as compared with their length, such as the small recess on a door frame, into which the edge of a door is made to fit, the recess of a brick jamb to receive a window frame, and the like. A joint formed by the rabbet(s) on one or both members; also rabbeted edge joint; rabbeted right angle joint.

Raceways: A channel used for the specific purpose of holding cables, busbars, and wires.

Rafraichissoir: (French) Refrigerator.

Rafter: A beam that serves to support the roof. It slopes from the eaves to the ridge of a roof.

Rail: A horizontal member in a door or window frame or panel. In carpentry, any horizontal member morticed or otherwise secured between or upon two posts, forming a frame or panel, as, first, in fencing, whether the closure is made by several parallel rails or by only two to give nailing to palings; second, as a coping to a balustrade, when it is called a hand rail; third, in panelling, doors, and the like, being the horizontal member of the frame in which the panels are set, the vertical members being the stiles. The rails of massive stone, elaborately sculptured, which form the ceremonial enclosures of ancient Buddhist topes, temples, etc., in India, are among the most characteristic and important features of Buddhist architecture.

Raised grain: Roughened condition of surface of dressed lumber on which hard summerwood is raised above the softer springwood, but is not torn loose from it.

Rake: Inclination or slope, as of a roof or of a flight of steps in a staircase.

Ramp: An inclined plane, as of a floor rising from a lower to a higher level, taking the place of steps; specifically, a concave connecting sweep in a vertical plane, as on a coping or hand rail, where it turns from a sloping to a horizontal direction, or rises from one level to a higher level. The part of a staircase handrail which rises at a steeper angle than normal.

Ram's head: A building and furniture design motif.

Random sheared: A carpet texture created by shearing either level loop or high-low loop carpet lightly so that only the higher loops are sheared. The sheared areas are less reflective than the unsheared loops which appear brighter and lighter in color. Random shearing of high-low loop carpet produces a texture somewhat similar to cut and loop.

Rapid start fluorescent lamp: A fluorescent lamp designed for operation with a ballast that provides a low-voltage winding for preheating the electrodes and initiating the arc without a starting switch or the application of high voltage.

Rattan: Furniture made from the Asian palm tree. The thin palm leaves are woven into baskets and furniture.

Raw footcandles: Same as footcandles. This term is sometimes used in order to differentiate between ordinary footcandles and ESI footcandles. (Footcandles or Raw Footcandles refers only to the quantity of illumination. ESI footcandles refers to task visibility by considering both the quantity and quality of illumination.)

Rayonnant: French Gothic style from about 1270 to about 1370.

Reading chair: An eighteenth century chair that had an adjustable ledge that could be used to read or write.

Recamier: A daybed that was backless and had uneven ends from the Empire-Directoire style.

Rectory table: A sixteenth century table that has four or more turned legs joined by stretchers. It is a thin and quite long dining table.

Redwood: A soft wood that is used for paneling and outdoor furniture. It is extremely durable and is grown almost exclusively in northern California.

Reed: (A) A type of molding. It is the long, thin stalk of tall grass. (B) Part of a carpet weaving loom consisting of thin strips of metal with spaces between them through which warp yarns pass. The motion of the reed pushes fill yarn tightly into the fabric.

Reed marks: Woven fabric (or woven carpet) defects consisting of lengthwise streaks caused by rubbing of reed elements against warp yarns.

Reflectance: Sometimes called reflectance factor. The ratio of reflected light to incident light (light falling on a surface). Reflectance is generally expressed in percent.

Reflected glare: Glare resulting from specular reflections of high luminances in polished or glossy surfaces in the field of view. It usually is associated with reflections from within a visual task or areas in close proximity to the region being viewed.

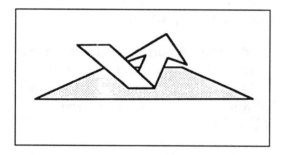

Reflection: Light striking a surface is either absorbed, transmitted, or reflected. Reflected light is that which bounces off the surface, and it can be classified as specular or diffuse reflection. Specular reflection is characterized by light rays which strike and leave a surface at equal angles. Diffuse reflection leaves a surface in all directions.

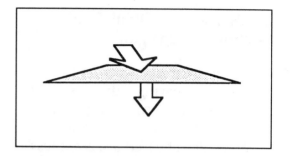

Refraction: The process by which the direction of a ray of light changes as it passes obliquely from one medium to another in which its speed is different.

Reignier work: Delicate woodwork of the nature of Marquetry, dating from the reign of Louis XIV, and named after a cabinetmaker of the time. It is not dissimilar to Boule Work.

Reinforced concrete: Concrete that has been reinforced by insertion of steel mesh or rods. This increases the tensile strength of the material which is inherently strong in compression and weak in tension.

Relief: That which is raised or embossed on a more or less uniform surface; raised work. A bold embossing is called high relief, *alto rilievo*; a low embossing is called low relief, or bas-relief, *basso rilievo*; a middle or half-relief is called *mezzo relievo*. In high relief the figures or objects represented project at least one half their natural rotundity or circumference from the background, parts of the figures sometimes being undercut and solid like statues, as in pediment sculpture; in low relief the projection of the figures is but slight, no part being entirely detached; a very flat relief, such as is seen on some coins, is called *stiacciato rilievo*. An Egyptian form of relief is counter sunk, i.e. it does not project above the general surface upon which it is wrought. This is known as *cavo rilievo* or *intaglio rilevato*; also hollow relief or *coelanaglyphic* sculpture. The outlines are incised, and the relief is thus contained in a sunk panel no bigger than itself. Relief work executed in thin metal may be done by *repousse* work, or by chasing; or may be copied by the electrotype process. Other relief in metal is done by casting. Relief work of the best periods did not represent its subject pictorially, and the surface upon which subject and action were depicted was recognized as the actual background, no attempt having been made at perspective illusions. But in later art, this proper condition of relief work was less uniformly respected, and as in the panels of the arch of Titus, and in those of the bronze gates of the Baptistry at Pisa, actual pictorial subjects were attempted with distant backgrounds.

Remnant: A short piece of carpet roll goods usually less than nine feet long.

Rep: Plain fabric with narrow ribs.

Repeat: The dimensions of the basic pattern unit in any type of patterned carpet including printed, woven, high-low tufted loop, cut and loop, etc. See Match for further discussion.

Replica: A copy of a piece of furniture during the time the original is produced.

Repousse work: Relief work in thin metal wrought by being beaten up with hammers on the reverse side; the art of modelling and decorating the surface of plaques or vessels of gold, silver, copper, or other thin malleable metals, by hammering the metal on the underside with special tools so as to bulge it in patterns of any desired ornamental character, forming reliefs on the upper side. In fine work the pattern thus raised is modified, dressed, and finished by placing the metal face uppermost upon a yielding bed and beating it back so as more clearly to define the subject and correct its outlines, and by chasing and engraving it.

Reproduction: A copy that is manufactured after the original.

Required accessible areas: Areas which must be functionally usable and physically accessible by physically disabled people.

Residential building: That part of any structure in which families or households live or in which sleeping and accessory accommodations are provided, including but not limited to dwellings, multiple-family dwellings, hotels, motels, dormitories and lodging houses.

Resilience: The inherent characteristic of a fabric, carpet as well as padding, to return to its original thickness or shape after being walked on or held down by weight.

Resin: A solid or viscous liquid, used as part or all of the film-forming phase of paints, varnishes, and lacquers.

Resist printing: A technique for producing colored patterns wherein carpet is first printed with colorless chemicals which alter the dye affinity of the printed areas. The printed areas in nylon carpet, for example, may be altered to be light dyeing and/or cationic dyeable relative to the untreated regular acid dyeable nylon. Subsequent piece dyeing in a dye beck with appropriate selected dyestuffs produces a colored pattern. In this fashion numerous colorways may be produced from a single print run.

Restretch: A carpet installation term used to describe carpet stretching performed subsequent to original installation to remove wrinkles, bubbles, or loose fit. Most restretching is caused by failure of the installer to adequately stretch the carpet during original installation. Restretching should be performed with power stretchers and not with knee kickers. This is true of all stretching operations in overpad tackless strip installations.

Retainers and deposits: A designer will charge a retainer before the job is started or the client is charged a flat consulting fee. The client will pay a deposit before the work is started and then pay the remaining sum on completion of the work.

Reveal: That portion of the jamb of an opening or recess which is visible from the face of the wall back to the frame or other structure which may be placed between the jambs. Thus, the windows of an ordinary brick building have usually reveals of some four inches; that being the width of each brick jamb visible outside of the window frames.

Rez-de-chaussee: (French) Ground floor.

Ribbon-back chair: A rococo style chair back that has a carved splat that resembles ribbons and bows.

Rinceau: (French) An ornamental design of foliage stems carved or painted on eighteenth century French furniture.

Ring, annual growth: The growth layer put on in a growth year.

Rise: (A) The vertical distance between two consecutive treads in a stair; sometimes, the entire height of a flight of stairs from landing to landing. (B) The vertical height of the curved part of an arch, that is the distance measured vertically, as in an elevation, from the springing line to the highest point of the curved intrados.

Riser: (A) The upright of one step, whether the step be in one piece as a block of stone, or built up. In the former case, the riser is the surface alone. In the latter case, the riser is the board, plate of cast iron, or similar thin piece which is set upright between two treads. (B) By extension, the same as Rise. A stair in which the treads are separate planks, slabs or slate, plates or iron, or the like, is sometimes built without risers. In this case, an incorrect extension of the term is used, and such a stair is said to have open risers.

R lamps: Reflectorized lamps available in spot (clear face) and flood (frosted face).

Rocaille: A system of decoration supposed to be founded upon the forms of rocks, or upon the artificial rock work of the seventeenth-century gardens to which were added shells sometimes of real, sometimes of imaginary shapes. The ornament soon passed into a system of scrolls combined with abundant floral and other carving, with gilding used freely, and paintings in panels. This system of ornamentation was used equally for the wood-lined interiors of handsome residences and choirs of churches, and for the smallest objects of familiar ornamentation, such as the little boxes of gold, ivory, and tortoise shell used for snuff and bon bons, small toilet articles and the like. The essence of the style is that these curves shall never be continuous for more than a short distance, nor make more than one double curve like the letter S, without breaking off to begin again abruptly.

Rockingham porcelain: Brown and white porcelain with a purple-brown glaze that was produced in Yorkshire around 1742.

Roll-top desk: A Hepplewhite desk that has a lid that can roll down to cover the work space.

Romex: A cable comprised of flexible plastic sheathing inside of which are two or more insulated wires for carrying electricity.

Roof: That part of the closure of a building which covers it in from the sky. Upon this part of a building depends in large measure the character of its design as a work of architecture. Roofs are distinguished: (1) By their form and method of construction; as, the flat roof, characteristic of dry tropical countries, and much used in modern commercial buildings in the United States; the sloping roof, including gables, hipped, penthouse, mansard, and gambrel roofs with their varieties. (2) By the character of their covering; as, thatched, shingled, battened, slated, tiles, metal-covered, tarred, asphalted, gravelled, etc. (A) In carpentry, the term refers to the timber framework by which the external surface is supported. This, in sloping roofs, consists usually of a series of pairs of opposite rafters or couples, of which the lower ends are tied together in various ways to prevent spreading; or, where the span is too great for such simple construction and there are no intermediate upright supports, of a series of rafters supported by longitudinal horizontal purlins, which are generally carried on a system of transverse timber frames or trusses, spaced from 8 to 20 feet apart. To suit various conditions of shape of roof and area to be covered, these typical and elementary forms are, in modern usage, subjected to innumerable structural modifications and extensions. One of the most marked distinctions in the historic styles consists in the pitch or inclination of the roof. Thus in the Greek temple the slope of the pediment varied from 15 degrees to 16 1/2 degrees; Roman roofs had a slope of from 22 degrees to 23 1/2 degrees; Romanesque roofs followed closely the Roman slope; the Gothic pitch was much steeper, sometimes reaching 50 degrees or even 60 degrees. In the Renaissance era there was in Italy a revival of the Roman pitch with the other classic features; but the French builders of this era retained the steepest slopes of the medieval sky lines, especially in the conical roofs of their round towers and in the pyramidal roofs with which they characteristically covered each separate division of their buildings. These lofty roofs, with their high dormers, chimneys, and crestings, constitute a distinctive characteristic of the French Renaissance, the peculiar steep roof being a development from these French traditions. The structural conditions from which the steep medieval pitch was evolved.

Room: An enclosure or division of a house or other structure, separated from other divisions by partitions; an apartment, a chamber; as a drawing-room, parlor, dining room, or chamber in a house, a stateroom in a ship or railroad car, a harness room in a stable.

Room Cavity Ratio: (RCR) A numerical relationship of the vertical distance between work plane height and luminaire mounting height to room width and length. It is used with the Zonal Cavity method of calculating average illumination levels.

Room divider: A device used to separate areas of a room. It can be a folding screen or a drapery etc.

Rope: A roll molding decorated with a twist like the strands of a rope, common in Romanesque architecture; a cable molding.

Rose: (A) A conventional representation of the flower in its original or wild state, much used in Gothic sculpture and especially in late English Gothic and Elizabethan art. One form of it is especially suggestive of English political changes, historically representing the revival of the houses of York and Landcaster. (B) A circular or nearly circular ornament. (C) A diaphragm of woven wire or of a plate of metal pierced with holes to stop solid matters which might clog a pipe.

Rosette: A pattern or design in the shape of a rose. Usually carved or inlaid.

Rotary brushing: A carpet cleaning technique in which a detergent solution is worked into the pile by a motor-driven rotating brush. Loosened soil and spent solution is often subsequently removed by vacuum.

Rotary brush machine: A carpet shampooing machine that feeds the cleaning solution through a bristled scrubbing brush mechanically driven on a plane parallel to the carpet.

Rouen faience: Fourteenth century earthenware made in Rouen France that is glazed with tin.

Rough Service Lamps:
Incandescent lamps designed with extra filament supports to withstand bumps, shocks and vibrations with some loss in lumen output.

Round wire or looped pile: A Wilton or velvet carpet woven with the pile yarn uncut. A looped surface pile tuft.

Roving: An intermediate stage in the production of spun yarns consisting of a loose assembly of staple fibers with little or no twist. Roving is smaller than sliver but larger than yarn.

Rows or wires: In woven carpet this is the number of pile yarn tufts per running inch lengthwise. Called rows in Axminster and wires in Wilton and velvet carpet. Analogous to stitches per inch in tufted carpet.

Royal Copenhagen: An eighteenth century Dutch hard-paste porcelain.

Royal Worcester: See Worcester china.

Rubber: A term sometimes applied to carpet cushion made from foam or sponge, and to both separate and attached cushions.

Rubber or vinyl backed carpet: The carpet construction can be either woven or tufted although most carpets of this type are of tufted construction in broadloom widths. When woven, they are usually manufactured in narrower widths up to 54 inches wide. Instead of the conventional type of secondary back, the manufacturer bonds a backing compound of either a high density foam rubber known as Hi-D, or sponge rubber made of a latex formula, or a vinyl composition. The thickness of this type of secondary back varies with the purpose for which the carpet is made. The above compounds, with the exception of sponge rubber, are applied in a more or less liquid state and then hardened and cured with heat. When sponge rubber is utilized, it is manufactured in a flat sheet form and bonded by means of an adhesive. The lamination is generally done by a company other than the carpet maker which makes it possible to obtain any type of carpet construction with a bonded rubber back.

Ruffle: A piece of fabric that has been gathered or pleated.

Rug: A soft floor covering not fastened to the floor and usually not covering the entire floor. Carpet cut into room or area dimensions and loose laid.

Running dog: A classical ornament resembling waves.

Rush seating: A chair seat that is woven with grasslike plants such as reeds or rushes.

Rustic furniture: Outside furniture made from cast iron, plastic, aluminum, cement or wood.

S

Saber leg: A chair leg that curves in a rearward fashion similar to a saber or sword.

Sailcloth: See canvas.

Salver: A silver tray that is flat and sits on mounted legs.

Sampler: An embroidered piece of needlework that is used as a pillow case or as a framed decoration.

Sanded, smoothly: Sanded sufficiently smooth so that sander marks will be concealed by painter's applied finish.

Sandwich glass: Glass that was produced from 1825-1886. It was either pressed, molded or blown and produced by the Sandwich Glass Company.

Sapwood: Wood occurring between the bark and the heart of the tree.

Saruk carpet: A Persian rug that is closely knotted with a deep pile.

Sash: A single assembly of stiles and rails into a frame for holding glass, with or without dividing.

Sateen: Satin-weave fabric of mercerized cotton.

Satin: Cloth with a dull back and glossy face. Made of silk, cotton or synthetics.

Satinwood: A hard wood light in color and used on fine furniture. It is very smooth and found in southern Asia.

Satsuma ware: A sixteenth century Japanese pottery that is yellow to brown and has a crackled glaze.

Satyr: An ornamental motif of a half man half goat mythological creature.

Sauna: A steam bath created by pouring hot water over hot rocks.

Savonarola chair: An X-shaped folding chair named for an Italian monk.

Savonnerie carpet: A Turkish style knotted pile carpet with French design.

Saxony: A cut-pile carpet texture consisting of heat-set plied yarns in a relatively dense, erect configuration, with well defined individual tuft tips. Saxonies are denser and have more erect tufts than shags. Their tip definition is more pronounced than in singles plush, which is another dense cut-pile carpet style. Saxonies have generally displaced singles plush styles from the market place, and many dealers call their smoother finished saxonies plushes.

Scale Drawing: A drawing, such as a building blueprint, having its measurements in fixed proportion to the actual dimensions of the room, floor, or building depicted. A typical scale might be one quarter inch to the foot. On such a drawing, each quarter inch of linear dimension represents one foot of linear dimension in the actual structure.

Scale rule: A drafting ruler that comes in triangular and flat styles, and in 6" and 12" lengths. 1/4" scale means that a foot in the actual building would be represented by 1/4" on the plan. The scale rule makes thinking in scale much easier, for in the 1/4" scale, the rule is marked just as if each 1/4" is a foot, and these "small" feet are broken into 12 "inches." Other scales like 1/8", 1/4", 1/2", 3/8", 1-1/2", and 3" are represented. A 12" triangular scale rule is the basic scale rule.

Scarf: The oblique joint by which the ends of two pieces of timber are united, long ends of two parts being usually cut with projections and

recesses which mutually fit one another, and these are sometimes forced together and tightened by keys or wedges in various ways, and secured by iron straps and bolts. Also the part cut away and wasted from each timber in shaping it to form this joint.

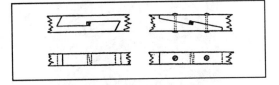

Scarf, end: One formed by the insertion of one end into the other in a manner approaching a mortice and tenon.

Scarf, hook butt: One in which the timbers form, in part, butt joints with one or more oblique cuts, by which they are hooked together.

Scratching: The roughening of the first coat of plaster, when fresh, by scratching or scoring its surface with a point so that the next coat may adhere to it more fimly.

Screed: A narrow strip of plastering brought to a true surface and edge, or a strip or bar of wood, to guide the workmen in plastering the adjoining section of the wall surface.

PERPENDICULAR.

OPEN TRACERY

In church architecture, specifically, a decorated pattern of wood, metal, or stone, closed or open, serving to separate, actually or in sentiment, a chapel from the church, an aisle from the nave or choir, the chancel from the nave, etc. In this sense, a screen replaces the jube in small churches. In early houses of some importance, a partition by which the entrance lobby is separated from the great hall. An open colonnade or arcade if serving to enclose a courtyard, or the like, is sometimes called a screen.

Scribe: To mark with an incised line, as by an awl; hence, to fit one piece to another of irregular or uneven form, as a plain piece against a molded piece, or as in shaping the lower edge of a baseboard to fit the irregularities of the floor.

Scribe cutting: Cutting the exact irregularities in one carpet edge to fit the contours of another carpet edge.

Scribing: An installation term for the method of transferring the exact irregularities of a wall, floor, or other surface onto a piece of carpet or other material by a tracing technique. The material is then cut to fit exactly.

Screen: Any structure of any material having no essential function of support and serving merely to separate, protect, seclude, or conceal.

Scrimshaw: Carved objects made from bone, shell or ivory.

Scroll: An ornament in the shape of a paper roll or scroll. The volute of an Ionic or Corinthian capital.

Scrutoire: (French) A slant-top desk, with a lid that opens to create a horizontal writing surface.

Sculpture: The technique of hand carving or chiseling animal, human, abstract or other forms out of marble, stone or clay.

Sculptured: A pattern in a carpet that is manufactured to simulate the effect of hand carving by eliminating or drawing down certain pile yarns tightly to the back to form a specific design on the face of the carpet. Any carpet pattern formed from high and low pile areas, such as high-low loop or cut-and-loop.

Sealer: A paint or varnish used to prevent excessive absorption of finish coats by a substratum; also used to prevent bleeding or bonding of chalked masonry surface when painting.

Seam finishing: The term that describes the process of bringing up erect any tufts trapped in a completed carpet seam followed by trimming with napping shears any protrusions in the seam level with the surrounding tufts.

Seat support system: The structural supporting system for loose seat cushions.

Secondary backing: Woven or non-woven fabric reinforcement laminated to the back of tufted carpet, usually with latex adhesive, to enhance dimensional stability, strength, stretch resistance, lay-flat stiffness, and hand. Most secondary backings are woven jute, woven polypropylene, or nonwoven polypropylene. The term is sometimes used in a broader sense to include attached cushion and other polymeric back coatings. Because secondary backing is visible, whereas primary backing is concealed under the pile yarn in finished carpet, most dealers and installers refer to the secondary backing simply as backing.

Seconds: Off-quality, defective, or substandard carpet normally marketed at substantial price discounts as seconds or imperfects by manufacturers. If manufacturers' first quality standards are high, seconds may represent excellent values.

Secretaire: (French) Desk.

Secretaire-a-abattant: (French) Drop-lid desk.

Section: (A) The surface or portion obtained by a cut made through a structure or any part of one, in such a manner as to reveal its structure and interior detail when the part intervening between the cut and the eye of the observer is removed. (B) The delineation of a section as above defined. In general scale drawings, sections usually represent cuts made through a structure on vertical planes, which are Plans.

Sectional furniture: Furniture pieces that are independent of one another but also match and can be arranged in several ways.

Securely attached: Attached by nails or screws, or by a groove or plow joint securely glued, forming a rigid assembly.

Self-ballasted mercury lamps: Any mercury lamp of which the current-limiting device is an integral part.

Self-edge: Application to the edge of plywood or particleboard of a plastic laminate of the same pattern as the face surface.

Self-Tone: A pattern of two or more shades of the same color. When two shades are used in a pattern or design, it is called two-tone.

Selvage: An edge of fabric or wallpaper that is woven to prevent raveling.

Selvages: Carpet edges at sides of rolls.

Semainier: (French) A tall bedroom chest. A chest that has seven drawers. It comes from the French word meaning week, and as there are seven days in a week there are seven drawers, one for each day.

Semigloss: Surface glossiness of a paint or finish that falls between eggshell and a high or full gloss.

Serging: A method of finishing edges of area rugs cut from roll goods by use by heavy colored yarn sewn around the edges in a close overcast stitch.

Servante: An Empire style serving table.

Service entrance: Point at which power utility wires enter a building.

Set match: Pattern repeats that are positioned or set side by side on the same level to form a straight line across the width of the fabric.

Setting: The process of preparing a pattern for the Axminster loom by winding the specified colored yarns on a spool in the sequence required for weaving.

Sevres ware: French porcelain that is soft paste and decorated with flowers or figures.

Sewing pole: Any piece of wood or other material, more or less rounded, over which carpet may be laid in order to facilitate sewing and other related operations. Most installers prefer a wooden pole about 4 inches in diameter that has been slightly flattened on one side.

Sewing table: A table where sewing can be done.

Sgraffito (graffito): (A) Decorative technique of exposing an undercoat of paint on pottery. (B) Plaster decorated with incised patterns. The top coat is cut to reveal a different colored undercoat.

Shading: Apparent color difference between areas of the same carpet caused by normal wear and the resulting random difference in pile lay direction. It is a characteristic of all cut-pile carpet and is most pronounced in singles plush. It is not a manufacturing defect. The physical cause is the difference between cut end, luster and side luster of fibers. The sides of fibers reflect more light and appear brighter and lighter in color than the ends which absorb more light and appear to be duller and darker in color. Bent cut pile fibers in a carpet or rug that cause reflected light to give the illusion of dark or light areas on the fabric.

Shaft-ring: A decorative ring around a shaft.

Shag: A carpet texture characterized by long pile tufts laid over in random directions in such a manner that the sides of the yarn form the traffic surface. Modern shags are made from plied heat-set yarns and are either cut-pile or cut-and-loop styles.

Shag carpets: This carpet is usually made on the tufting machine. It is fabricated with cut pile tufts spaced wider apart than normal so that they lay over in random directions. The resulting tumbled, shaggy appearance of the pile gives this type of carpet its popular name. In some fabrics of this type, the extra long pile tufts are spaced a bit closer together to achieve a plush look and feel, commonly called Splash, a contraction of the words Shag and Plush. It is manufactured in a variety of pile heights and is available in solid colors as well as moresque pile.

Shake: A separation of the wood, normally between growth rings.

Shaker furniture: Furniture in the style or made by the Shaker religious community. A substantially extinct group that flourished in the Eastern and Mid-Western U.S.

Shearing: Carpet manufacturing process for producing a smooth carpet face, removing fuzz, or creating random sheared textures. Carpet shears have many steel blades mounted on rotating cylinders which cut fibers on carpet surfaces in a manner analogous to a lawn mower cutting grass. Depth of shearing may be indicated by a modifying word, e.g., defuzz and tipshear suggest a shallow cut of the shear, whereas a full shear would imply a deep cut as used for producing mirror-finished plush.

Sheathing: A covering of boards, plywood or paneling etc. applied to the exterior rafters, joists or studs to strengthen the structure. In carpentry, a covering or lining to conceal a rough surface or to cover a timber frame. In general, any material, such as tin, copper, slate, tiles, etc., prepared for application to a structure, as covering.

Shed: A weaving term describing the space between warp yarns (created by alternate raising and lowering of the loom harness) in which the fill yarn is carried by the shuttle or other fill insertion device.

Sheetrock: Gypsum plasterboard placed between paper.

Shell: (A) A furniture design motif. (B) A thin self-supporting member.

Shellac: A wood finisher and resin used in varnish.

Shield-back chair: A chair that has an open back resembling a shield.

Shielding: An arrangement of light-controlling material to prevent direct view of the light source.

Shielding angle (of a luminaire): The angle from the horizontal at which a light source first becomes visible. It is the complementary angle of the cut-off angle. In the case of a luminaire shielded by a reflector or parabolic cell louver, it is important to ascertain also the shielding angle to the reflected image of the light source, as this is often almost as bright as the source itself.

Shim: A piece of wood used to balance a piece of furniture.

Shingle: Originally, a thin parallelogram of wood (in the United States generally 6"x 18"- 24"), split and shaved, and more recently sawn, thicker at one end than the other; used for covering sides or roofs of houses, about 4 or 5 inches of its length being exposed. Shingles are now sometimes made of metal in the form of tiles.

Shingle style: An American residential building style from the 1870's and 1880's.

Shiplap: A joint that overlaps and joins two boards.

Shoe: A piece of stone, timber, or, more commonly, of iron, shaped to receive the lower end of any member; either to protect the end, as in the case of a pile which is to be driven into hard ground, or to secure the member at its junction with another. In this case, commonly adapted to prevent the penetration or rupture of one member by the other, as in the case of a plate under the end of a post or under the nut of a tie rod.

Shoji: A Japanese partition or screen, usually covered with rice paper.

Shooting or sprouting: Emergence of long pile tufts above the normal pile surface. The condition is often correctable by cutting the sprouted tufts even with the pile with a scissors or knife before or after installation.

Short roll: A length of carpet roll goods shorter than a full shipping roll and longer than a remnant. Usually sold by carpet mills at substantial discounts from first quality full roll mill prices, but higher than second quality prices.

Shot: (A) A weaving term for fill yarn, the yarn inserted at right angles to the warp across the fabric width. In woven carpet, it is the number of picks of fill yarn per row of pile tufts. (B) The number of weft yarns for each row of pile tufts crosswise on the loom.

Should: Wording used in a design specification when an instruction is advised but not required.

Shrink: The natural contraction of wood that hasn't been correctly dried.

Shuttle: Part of a weaving loom which carries fill yarn back and forth across the fabric width. In conventional looms it contains a spool of fill yarn called a bobbin.

Sideboard: A table that has drawers and sits against a wall intended to be used as a server.

Side chair: An office guest or dining chair which often sits beside a table or desk.

Side seams: Also known in the industry as length seams. Those seams running the length of the carpet.

Side table: A table that is long and narrow and used a server.

Siding: The covering, or material for covering, the exterior walls of a frame building, and forming the final finished surface, as distinguished from the sheathing, on which, when used, the siding is nailed.

Silk: Fibers made from silkworm cocoon extrusions. Fabric made from silk fibers.

Silk-screening: A process in which a stenciled design is imposed on a screen that is stretched on a frame. One color is used on a screen and the ink is forced through the cloth.

Sill: A horizontal member at the base of a framed wall or at the bottom of a door frame or window opening.

Silvered bowl lamps: Incandescent A lamps with a silver finish inside the bowl portion of the bulb. Used for indirect lighting and glare reduction.

Single Hung: Secured to one side or at one point only, as a sash which is hung by one cord, pulley, and weight. This plan is followed where a window is divided by a mullion which for any reason is to be made as slender as possible. A solid mullion being put in place, the two sliding sashes are each hung on the outer edge along, the single weight being heavy enough to counterbalance the sash. It is usually necessary to insert rollers of some kind in the other stile of each sash to prevent their binding or sticking.

Sisal: A fiber used to make cord and rope having great strength.

Size, sizing: A wall sealer used before applying wall paper.

Skein dyeing: Skein dyeing employs very much the same principle as stock dyeing. The difference lies in the prior spinning of the fibers into single strands of yarn and then gathering them into hanks or skeins, of yarn. The skeins replace the batches of raw stock, but the dyeing process remains the same. After washing and drying, the dyed single yarns in the skeins are plied into finished yarns.

Sketch: A simple drawing of something not giving exact details.

Sketching: The free hand drawing, more or less in proportion, of the details of an area, object, etc.

Skirt: (A) A piece of fabric hanging from the bottom of furniture to the ground. (B) An apron-piece or border, as the molded piece under a window stool, or the plinth board or mopboard of a room or passage, which last is in the United States called base or baseboard.

Skylight: A glazed aperture in a roof, whether a simple glazed frame set in the plane of a roof, or a structure surmounting a roof with upright or sloping sides and perhaps an independent roof; the entire structure consisting wholly, or in large part, of glazed frames. In its more elaborate forms, a skylight may be constructed as a Lantern, or may have the semblance of a dormer window from which it is sometimes hardly to be distinguished. The term is, however, only applicable to such lights when overhead, i.e. located decidedly above, rather than at the sides of, the space immediately covered by the roof, although, perhaps, extending considerably down the lateral slopes of the roof. The frame is either of wood, or, preferably, of metal, braced or ties with iron rods, if of large size, the metal sash bars being shaped with gutters to carry off the water of condensation, and glazed with sheets of fluted or rough plate glass, varying from 12" x 48" 3/16 to 20" x 100" 6/16 of an inch thick; if ordinary double thick glass is used, the sheets are from 9 to 15 inches wide, and from 16 to 30 inches long. In metal sash bars or mountings these sheets are set without putty. Skylights are often provided with ventilators arranged to be opened or closed by cords from below, and a flat decorated inner skylight is frequently placed beneath the outer skylight in a ceiling panel, when it is desired to make this feature an element in an architectural composition as seen from beneath. Sometimes, as in the covering of interior courts, winter gardens, exposition buildings, conservatories, marquises or canopies, and horticultural buildings, the entire roof is a skylight, and is emphasized as an especial architectural feature, the frame in such cases being of iron or wood. Occasionally smaller skylights are in the form of glazed scuttles arranged to be opened for access to the roof.

Slat-back chair: A chair whose back has slender pierced slats evenly spaced. It was first popular in the seventeenth century.

Sleepy Hollow chair: A chair that has a high back that continues into the seat.

Sleigh bed: A bed with a scrolled headboard and a footboard that is lower, thus resembling a horse-drawn sleigh.

Slipper chair: An eighteenth and nineteenth century chair with short legs.

Slip seat: A seat that is upholstered and fits into the frame of a chair.

Sliver: An intermediate stage in the production of spun yarns from staple fiber. It is a large, soft, untwisted strand or rope of fibers produced by carding or pin drafting.

Smoldering: Combustion without flame. It may burn for a long time and generate smoke, toxic gases, and heat.

Smolder resistance: Materials in which nonflaming combustion is inhibited or prevented.

Snakewood: See zebrawood.

Sofa table: A table with drop end leaves that was placed in front of a sofa.

Sofa: A piece of furniture that holds three people or more, is upholstered and usually found in the living or family room.

Soffit: The under side of a structure, especially of comparatively limited extent. Thus the under side of an arch or lintel and the sloping surface beneath a stair would be called soffits.

Soft-paste porcelain: Porcelain that uses less heat to be fused thus making it soft paste.

Softwood: Wood that comes from pine or spruce, coniferous trees and is not often used to make furniture.

Soil retardant: A chemical finish applied to fibers or carpet and fabric surfaces which inhibits attachment of soil to fiber.

Solder: An alloy of varying composition, but always easily fusible, employed in joining pipes or surfaces. Solder for making wiped joints in lead pipe consists of three parts lead and two parts tin.

Solution dyed: Describes a method that dyes man-made fibers while they are in liquid form before they become solid strands of yarn. The dye then becomes part of the fiber.

Sopraporta: A painting above the door of a room.

Sound Transmission Class: (STC) A number rating system for room to room sound transmission through air handling luminaries. The higher the STC number, the lower the level of sound transmission.

Space dyed: Yarn dyed two or more colors which alternate along the length. Space dyeing is a technique that applies different colors side by side on the same piece of yarn. One process frequently used applies the colors by running many parallel yarns through printing rollers. Then the yarns are steamed to set the colors, washed and dried before winding. Another space dyeing method prints the dyes on both sides of a sheet or tube of yarns which have been knitted together. After dyeing, the sheets or tubes of yarns are steamed, washed, and dried. Then the yarns are unravelled and the individual yarns are ready for tufting or weaving. This technique is known as knit-deknit.

Space planning: The functional planning of interior space. A design specialty practiced by interior designers and architects which concentrates on establishing space needs and utilization in the early or preliminary stages of design.

Spacing Ratio: (S.R.) The ratio of the distance between luminaire centers to the height above the work plane. The maximum spacing ratio for a particular luminaire is determined from the candlepower distribution curve for that luminaire and, when multiplied by the mounting height above the work plane, gives the maximum spacing of luminaries at which even illumination will be provided.

Spar varnish: A varnish that is resistant to salt, sun and water.

Species: A distinct kind of wood.

Spectral Energy Distribution (SED) Curves: A plot of the level of energy at each wavelength of a light source.

Sphere Illumination: The illumination on a task from a source providing equal luminance in all directions about that task, such as an illuminated sphere with the task located at the center.

Spike roll: Part of a tufting machine that pulls the primary backing and tufted carpet through the working area of the machine. It consists of a pinned driven roll that grips the cloth. The relationship of spike roll rotational speed and strokes per minute of the needle bar determines the number of stitches per inch in the tufted product.

Spindle-back chair: A chair whose back has two rows of vertical spindles.

Spinet: A harpsichord with one keyboard.

Spinning: A term for yarn or fiber production. To the fiber manufacturer, spinning is synonymous with extrusion of polymer through the small holes of the spinneret into synthetic fiber. To the conventional textile yarn mill, spinning is the conversion of staple fiber into spun yarn.

Spinning wheel: A machine used to spin cotton, wool or flax into thread. It was used until the nineteenth century.

Splat: A vertical member on a chair back.

Spline: A joint formed by the use of a spline. A spline is a thin, narrow strip, usually of plywood, inserted into matching grooves which have been machined in abutting edges of panels or lumber to insure a flush

alignment and secure joints. Customarily runs the entire length of the joint.

Split: A separation of the wood due to the tearing apart of the wood cells. (A) A very short split is approximately as long as one-half the width of the piece. (B) A short split is approximately as long as the width of the piece.

Splush: A tufted carpet style, no longer popular, combining characteristics of both shag and plush textures. Most splushes were made from nonheat-set singles yarns (similar to yarns used in plush) but were constructed with long pile length on wide gauge machines at relatively low stitch rates (similar to shag construction). The combination of singles yarns and low density tuft placement resulted in matting, pilling, and generally poor wear performance. It is definitely not a contract style.

Sponge cushion: A carpet cushion which is made of chemically blown sponge, it may have either a waffle or flat surface.

Spool furniture: Furniture that has spool turnings for legs and arms.

Spoon-back chair: An eighteenth century chair that had a back developed to fit the spine.

Sprinkler: A system of perforated pipes extending through a building, and at frequent points connected with a water supply controlled by fusible plugs which, when melted by an accidental fire in their neighborhood, automatically turn on the water and start the sprinklers to extinguish the flames.

Sprouting: The appearance of pile ends protruding above the surface of a new rug or carpet. It is caused by long ends of pile tufts which were not clipped during the manufacturer's shearing process. May be clipped with scissors. See Shooting.

Spun dyed: Same as Solution Dyed and Dope Dyed.

Spur: A decoration placed at the transition of a square plinth to a circular pier.

Square, T: A drafter's square, having a long blade attached at about the center of a shorter crosspiece. In use, the latter is moved along the edge of a drawing board, holding the long blade in successive parallel positions. Some T squares have adjustable blades, which can be set at different angles with the head.

Staffordshire: A county in England where bone china and clay pottery were manufactured.

Stain: (A) A coloring liquid or dye for application to any material--most often wood. It differs from paint as being thinner and readily absorbed by the pores of the material, instead of forming a coating on the surface, so that the texture and grain of the material is not concealed. In America stain has been used for exteriors of frame houses, the shingles and clapboards taking on a rougher and far more picturesque look than if painted. (B) Any ingredient which is used to change the color of a material by chemical action, as in the case of glass, in which a deep blue is got by means of protoxide of cobalt, and a green by copper and by iron, as in the production of pot metal. Silver Stain is more properly an enamel applied to the surface without changing the color of the mass.

Stained glass: Glass that is chemically treated and then fired to achieve the desired color.

Staircase: A series of stairs that have a rail and a frame.

Stairway: Three or more risers constitute a stairway.

Standard design: Any buildings, system, model, series, or component intended for duplication or repetitive construction or manufacture.

Standard fabric: Fabrics that conform to the minimum performance characteristics of their respective class.

Standard roll: The standard unit of measure for wall covering, 36 sq. ft.

Staple fiber: Short lengths of fiber which may be converted into spun yarns by textile yarn spinning processes. Also simply called staple. Staple may also be converted directly into non-woven fabrics such as needle-punched carpet. For carpet yarns spun on the common modified worsted systems, most staple is six to eight inches long. Fibers in their natural state before they are spun into yarns.

Static Shock: Discharge of electrostatic potential from carpet to person to conductive ground, e.g., a doorknob. Shoe friction against carpet fiber causes production of electrostatic charge. Various static control systems and finishes are used in contract carpet to dissipate

static charge before it builds to the human sensitivity threshold.

Statuary bronze: An acid finish applied to bronze statues.

Stay tacking: A carpet installation term for temporary nailing or tacking to hold the stretch until the entire installation is stretched over and fastened onto the tackless strip. An important technique in large contract installations which are too large to stretch in one step.

Steam cleaning: A carpet cleaning process that forces a pressurized mist of a solution of a detergent and hot, warm, or cold water into the carpet pile and then extracts the dirty solution and most of the moisture.

Steel furniture: Furniture that became popular in the eighteenth and nineteenth centuries. Chairs, beds and tables were made.

Stenciling: A process of color application onto another material through a heavy water proof template.

Step return: Also known as a bullnose. A bottom step with its tread frequently wider and longer than the rest of the steps in the flight and usually rounded at one or both ends.

Steuben glass: Glass that is iridescent and often designed by artist's for the Stueben Glass Works Company.

Stiffness: Resistance of materials, such as carpet, to bending.

Stile: Any plane surface forming a border. Specifically, in carpenter work and in joinery, one of the plane members of a piece of framing, into which the secondary members or rails are fitted by mortise and tenon, as in panelling. In framed doors, and the like, it is nearly always a vertical member.

Stile liberty: The Italian term for Art Nouveau.

Stitches per inch: Similar to wires per inch in a woven carpet, it indicates the number of rows of pile tufts per inch as measured along the length of a tufted carpet. The higher the number, then the more stitches per inch and the closer the pile rows are to each other down the length of the carpet.

Stitch Length: Total length of yarn from which a tuft is made. It is numerically equal to twice the pile height plus the associated back-stitch behind the primary backing.

Stock dyed yarn: Colored spun yarn produced from fibers dyed in staple form. The term does not include yarns spun from solution dyed staple. In this process, 500 to 1,000 pound batches of raw stock carpet fibers are immersed in pressurized bats through which heated dyes are circulated. To insure an even dye lot, 25,000 pounds or more of raw fibers are dyed in batches in this manner. Some dyers use a modification of this technique. A continuous process, similar to a production line feeds the batch of raw fibers through a dye bath. The dyed stock then goes to a steaming chamber to set the dye. Then it is washed free of any residual material and finally dried ready for spinning.

Stone china: An English china similar to ironware.

Stool: A seat that has no legs or arms and intended for one person.

Stop-chamfer: The decorative termination of a chamfer.

Stop marks: Widthwise mechanical pile imperfections in tufted carpet. Usually caused by improper stop and start techniques by the machine operator.

Straightedge: (A) A ruler used by draughtsmen for ruling long lines for which the T-square cannot be conveniently employed; e.g. the converging lines of a large perspective drawing. It is usually of light, hard wood, but hard rubber and celluloid are also used. (B) An implement used in building, for various purposes. For laying off long lines and for testing the evenness of a plane surface of plaster or stone, a thoroughly seasoned board with an edge planed perfectly true is employed. For testing levels a long, wide board is used, having the lower edge perfectly true and the middle part of the back or upper edge parallel to it; from this part the back tapers somewhat to either end. It is used by setting the lower edge on the surface or surfaces to be tested, and applying the spirit-level to the middle of the back.

Strapwork: A decoration of interlacing bands used in ceilings and screens.

Streak: Any lengthwise narrow visual defect in carpet. Dye streaks may be caused by a single pile end having different dye affinity from the others. Other streaks may be

yarn defects such as tight twist, stretched yarn or yarns larger or smaller than the others.

Stretch: A carpet installation term for the amount of elongation of carpet when it is stretched over cushion onto tackless strip. Generally one to two percent.

Stretching: A wall to wall carpet installation technique that stretches the carpet sufficiently to anticipate its future growth due to heat, humidity and traffic.

Strike-off: A sample of a paper of fabric design.

Stud: (I.) A relatively small projecting member as a boss, a small knob, a salient nailhead; either for ornamental or mechanical purpose.

Stud: (II.) Vertical framing members for interior and exterior wall construction. Often 2x4s of wood or metal.

Studio: (A) The working room of an artist, preferably arranged --in north latitude, --to receive north light and especially free from cross lights. (B) By extension from the above, any large apartment fitted as a working room, especially for more or less artistic employments, as photography and designing of all sorts.

Style: (I.) Character; the sum of many peculiarities, as when it is said that a certain building is in a spirited style. By extension, significance, individuality; especially in a good sense and imputed as a merit, as in the expression, Such a building has style.

Style: (II.) A peculiar type of building, of ornament, or the like, and constituting a strongly marked and easily distinguished group or epoch in the history of art; thus we say that in Europe the Romanesque style prevailed from the fall of the Western Empire until the rise of the Gothic style; but we also say that during the Romanesque period such minor styles as the Latin style, the Rhenish or West German style, the Norman Romanesque style, more vigorous in England than even in the country of its origin, and the Tuscan round-arched style, as in the church of Samminiato al Monte, were all in existence successively, or at the same time.

Subflooring: A rough base for a finished floor which rests on joists.

Suede cloth: Fabric made to resemble suede.

Surcharge: An extra charge added to the purchase price when less than the minimum is bought.

Surface check: The separation of a wood, normally occurring across the rings of annual growth, usually as a result of seasoning, and occurring only on one surface of the piece. (A) A fine surface check is not longer than 4". (B) A small surface check is over 4" and not longer than 6". (C) A medium surface check is over 6" but not longer than 8" surface, without any gaps.

Swag: A festoon formed like a draped cloth over supports.

Swatch: A small carpet sample. Carpet specifiers should retain swatches to verify color, texture, weight and other quality factors when carpet is delivered.

Swell front: See bow front.

T

T & G: Tongue-and-groove joint.

Table: (A) A flat distinctive, rectangular surface on a wall, often charged with inscriptions, painting, or sculpture; if raised, it is called a raised or projecting table; if rusticated in any way, a rusticated table; if raking, a raking table, etc. (B) A string course, or other horizontal bank of some size and weight. (C) In medieval architecture, the frontal on the face of an altar; the painted or carved panel behind and over an altar. (D) A slab set horizontally and carried on supports at a height of from 2 to 3 feet. In architectural treatment especially, (1) That used for the communion service when for any reason the altar is not in use, as at the time of the Puritan revolution in England, and as kept in usage by many sects of Christians; called Communion Table; Holy Table. (2) One of those used by the wealthier people of Roman antiquity for out-of-door service, composed usually of a slab of fine marble set upon carved marble supports. (3) One of those used in modern times for ornament rather than for use, as in the halls of the Pitti Palace at Florence, the tops of those being composed of great slabs of Florentine mosaic, or of some costly and rare natural material, such as one which is entirely of lapis lazuli, and one which is veneered with malachite; the frames of these being of carved and often gilded wood.

Table-a-ecran: (French) A table with a sliding screen.

Table-a-jeu: (French) Game table.

Table-a-l'anglaise: (French) An extension dining room table.

Table-a-l'architect: (French) A table with a hinged top.

Table-de-chevet: (French) Night table.

Table-jardiniere: (French) A table with a top pierced for plant containers.

Tabouret: (French) Stool.

Tack down installation: A method of installing wall to wall carpeting by tacking down the edges of the carpet.

Taffeta: Lightweight lustrous fabric made of silk, cotton, wool, acetate or rayon.

Tak dyeing: A continuous dyeing process for producing random multicolor patterns which are usually less sharply defined than printed patterns. Colored dye liquor is applied to the carpet in a controlled pattern of droplets.

Tallboy: An eighteenth century chest with two narrow drawers on the top and six wide drawers on the bottom.

Tall-case clock: See grandfather clock.

Tambour front: A wooden sliding door found on desks.

Tap down: One of the edge finishing moldings used to prevent unravelling and wear of the ends of a carpet. Also known as "clamp down".

Tapestry: (A) A hand worked fabric used for wall hangings. They usually have an image designed on them. (B) A single-weave yarn-dyed fabric made on a Jacquard loom.

Task: That which is to be seen. The visual function to be performed.

Task lighting: Lighting directed to a specific surface or area that provides illumination for visual tasks.

Tatami: A Japanese mat used as a standard unit of measurement in a room.

Tea caddy: An eighteenth century box used to hold tea. Tea caddies have partitions and are lined.

Teak: A hard wood medium brown in color found in the Orient. It resists moisture and is used mainly for furniture making.

Tear strength: Resistance to the propagation of an existing tear.

Technical pen: The basic ink drawing instrument. It is easy to use and comes in many line widths for various needs. It produces a uniform line width. A good basic set would include a 00 (very fine), 0, 2 1/2, then add 000, 1, 2, and 4. 00 is a good sketching instrument to use when a drafter occasionally needs to draft lines in ink for presentations and the like.

Tenon: Projecting tongue-like part of a wood member to be inserted into a slot (mortice) of another member to form a mortice and tenon joint. See Mortice and Tenon.

Tensile strength: The breaking strain of yarns or fabrics. A high tensile strength indicates strong yarns or fabrics.

Tented ceiling: Draping fabric on the walls and ceiling giving the effect of being in a tent.

Term: A tapering pedestal supporting a bust.

Terra cotta: Hard baked pottery, especially that which is used in architecture or in decorative art of large scale. It may be left with its natural brown surface unglazed and uncolored, or it may be painted as was customary among the Greeks, or it may be covered with a solid enamel of grave or brilliant colors. In parts of Italy the architecture of the later Gothic style and of the early Renaissance is marked by the free use of terra cotta. In the nineteenth century its use was largely revived, and in England from 1860, and in the United States from about 1880, it has been freely employed in connection with bricks of similar or agreeable contrasting color for the exterior of buildings, almost to the exclusion of cut stone.

Terrazzo: Marble chips mixed with cement mortar on site then ground and polished. Used as a flooring material.

Tesser: One small piece of a mosaic.

Tester: A canopy suspended over a pulpit, throne, bed, etc. A four poster bed canopy.

Tete-a-tete: An eighteenth century settee made for two people.

Texture: Visual and tactile surface characteristics of carpet pile including such esthetic and structural elements as high-low or cut-and-loop patterning, yarn twist, pile erectness or lay-over, harshness or softness to the touch, luster, and yarn dimensions.

Texturizing: See Bulking.

Thermal conductivity: Ability of a material to transmit heat. It is the reciprocal of resistivity. Good insulators, including some carpets, have high resistivity (R-value) and low thermal conductivity.

Thermoforming: Thermoplastic sheets are heated to a formable state and shaped to a mold. Air pressure may range and is evacuated between the sheet and the mold. This is vacuum forming.

Thermoplastic fabrics: Materials such as vinyl, olefin, polyester and nylon, which become soft or moldable when heat is applied.

Thick and thin yarns: Specialty yarns which vary in thickness.

Three-coat work: Plastering put on in three coats; superior to two-coat work. Ordinarily, in three-coat work the first coat is rough mortar, the second is scratched, that is to say, scored with the trowel so as to enable the finishing coat to hold to it more firmly, and the third is the finishing coat, which may be of sand finish or white finish.

Three-quarter carpet: A woven carpet term for narrow goods 27 inches wide.

Three-way lamps: Incandescent lamps that have two separately switched filaments permitting a choice of three levels of light such as 30/79/100, 50/100/150 or 100/200/300 watts. They can only be used in the base down position.

Threshold: The raised board beneath a door. Also known as sill or saddle.

Ticking: Tightly woven herringbone or twill cotton or linen fabric.

Tie-dye: A fabric that is tied together and dipped in various dyes giving a streaked effect.

Tiffany glass: Glass made by Louis Comfort Tiffany that is stained or iridescent. Louis Tiffany revived stained glass as an art form.

Tight seat: A fixed or unremovable upholstered furniture seat or cushion.

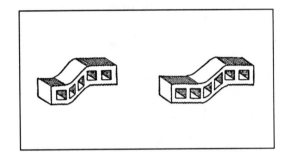

Tile: (A) Primarily, a piece of solid material used for covering a roof of a building. Roof tiles may be either flat or may be of different sections, so as to produce ridges and valleys, and so that one form covers the joints between tiles of another form, as will be explained below. (B) Any slab of hard material, large or small, but especially one of many rather small pieces, used together to form roofing, flooring, wall facing, or the like. Much the greater number of tiles have always been made of baked clay in some form; but marble, stone, and other materials are used. (C) By extension, and because of the application of the name to all pieces of baked clay used for accessories to building, a piece of drain pipe; one section of a continuous tube. In this sense often called Draining Tile or Drain Tile. (D) A piece of hard material, especially of baked clay, used for any purpose whatever, even for the preserving of written records, as in the case of those libraries entirely composed of inscribed tiles which have been found in Mesopotamia.

Timing: Operational sequence of the moving parts of looms and tufting machines.

Tip shearing: Light, shallow shearing to add surface interest to carpet texture or simply to clean up and defuzz during carpet finishing. Toile de Jouy: Plain or twill cotton fabric common in eigteenth and nineteenth century France.

Tole: (French) Painted tin or sheet metal.

Tone on tone: A carpet pattern made with two or more shades of the same hue.

Tongue: A projecting member, as a tenon; a continuous ridge left on the edge of a board or plank, and intended to fit into a groove worked in the edge of another board of plank. The joint so made is in constant use in flooring, and is used

occasionally in the siding of houses. Tongued and grooved flooring is objected to by some because, when heavy pressure comes at a point near the edge of a plank, one side of the groove may break away and the floor be permanently injured.

Torchere: A floor length lamp also an eighteenth century candle stand.

Total weight: Weight per square yard of the total carpet including the pile, yarn, primary and secondary backings, and coatings.

Tracings: In times past, architects paid people to make tracings of their original drawings to give to the contractors. This process was supplanted by the blueprinting process and left us with the term tracing which is still used to describe that original drawing on translucent paper. The blueprinting process itself has since been largely replaced by a much more inexpensive process called *Diazo*.

Traffic: The passing to-and-fro of persons with special reference to carpet wear resulting therefrom.

Transfer molding: This process is similar to compression molding but the plastic is heated to flexibility before it reaches the mold. It is forced into the mold by a hydraulic plunger.

Transmission: Vibrations that are propagated through various media.

Transom: A hinged window found over a door or another window. A horizontal bar across a window opening or panel. A horizontal bar of stone, metal, or wood, as distinguished from a Mullion; especially one across a door or window opening near the top.

Tread: (A) That part of a step in a stairway, of a doorsill, or the like, upon which the foot rests, as distinguished from the riser. The term applied equally to the upper surface along, and to the plank, slab of marble or slate, or thin casting of iron, in those staircases which each step is not a solid mass. (B) The horizontal distance from one riser to the next. Thus, a stair is said to have 12 1/2" tread, that being the whole distance which a person moves horizontally in ascending one step. This distance is measured without regard to the nosing, which, where is exists, projects beyond the riser in each case.

Trench header duct: An accessible type of floor outlet covered with a flat metal plate. After removing the plate, the duct is used for telephone connections, provide additional electrical outlets, make repairs and other service needs.

Trestle table: A medieval table with a stretcher and truss and end supports. It is narrow and used for dining.

Triangle: A drawing instrument in the form of a mathematical right-angled triangle cut from a flat thin piece of wood, hard rubber, celluloid, or metal, or framed of three strips; used for drawing parallel lines at any given angle by sliding it along the fixed blade of a T-square, straight edge, or the like. The right-angled side serves for lines perpendicular to the blade, the oblique side for inclined lines. The most common forms of a triangle have acute angles both of 45 degrees or one of 30 degrees and one of 60 degrees; but special forms are made with other angles for lettering and other special purposes. Called also Set Square.

Trimmer: A cutting tool used by the installer to cut off the excess carpet in a tackless installation and yet leave a predetermined amount of the cut edge to turn into the gully.

Tripod table: A table with three crossing legs.

Triptych: A hinged three paneled altarpiece that has a religious story painted on it.

Trivet: A stand that was used near a fireplace to keep a kettle warm. It has three legs and was usually made of metal.

Trompe l'oeil: A painting that gives the illusion of being three dimensional. It is the French term meaning fool the eye.

Trophy: A group of sculptured arms commemorating a victory.

Trowel: A notched steel tool designed to help the installer to spread predetermined sized ridges of adhesive on surfaces when adhering carpet.

Trumeau: (French) Panelling over a mantel or door, usually with a mirror superimposed with a picture.

Trundle or truckle bed: A bed that will fold down and roll under another bed.

T-Square: A drafting tool used to draw lines parallel to the drawing board front edge. It is snuggled tightly against the drawing board edge and the pencil is drawn across the plastic edge to make a straight and parallel line. Angled and perpendicular lines are constructed with a triangle. A wooden T-square with a clear plastic edge is the preferred one for drafting.

Tub chair: See barrel chair.

Tudor flower: A floral ornament common in late Gothic architecture.

Tudor style: A style of furniture from 1485-1558. Gothic forms of arches, ceiling, beams and carvings were popular.

Tuft bind: Force required to pull a tuft from the carpet (usually measured in ounces). The manufactured degree of resistance to pulls of the surface yarns.

Tufted: A surface treatment created by buttons which are laced through an upholstery fabric filling.

Tufted carpet: A tufting machine operates like a giant sewing machine containing hundreds of needles side by side. A suitable pile yarn is threaded through the eye of each of the needles. Then the multitude of needles, moving simultaneously, pushes the yarns through a previously constructed primary backing sheet either prewoven of jute or polypropylene, or a nonwoven sheet of natural or synthetic fibers. Loopers in the machine move close to each needle eye and engage the yarn. As each needle is pulled out, a loop of yarn or tuft is formed and held in place in the backing material. The looped pile may be left uncut, or the loops may be totally cut to form a surface plush effect or they may be selectively sheared into a surface texture of cut and loop in a variety of solid colors, tweeds, or stripes. In addition, the tufting machinery can produce high-low loops as well as sculptured effects. Colorful designs can be printed over the surface or randomly placed. Next, the backing material is coated with a compound which anchors the pile yarns permanently in place in the backing. This coating compound may be either of latex or thermoplastic. Then, a secondary backing sheet is applied over the first and both materials are laminated together by the same compound which then is cured. The secondary back adds both strength and body to the fabric as well as improves the stress and strain characteristics of the carpet. It adds dimensional stability. This secondary back may consist of the materials previously described, or, it may be a predetermined thickness of high density foam rubber, sponge rubber, vinyl, polyurethane or other compounds. Tufted carpets are usually manufactured in 12 and occasionally in 15 foot widths. More

than ninety 90% of all carpet sold in the United States is tufted.

Tufts: The cut or uncut loops of a pile fabric.

Tuft setting: The replacement of missing pile tufts in tufted carpet.

Tungsten-halogen lamp: A gas filled tungsten incandescent lamp containing a certain proportion of halogens.

Turkish rug: A fourteenth century rug having angular designs and warm colors. They were made in Asia Minor and were used as prayer rugs and wall hangings.

Turn and tack: A type of wall to wall installation similar to tack down except for turning under the edges of the carpet prior to tacking down through both thicknesses.

Tweed: Coarse twill or herringbone weave wool fabric with two or more color yarns.

Twist: (A) A distortion caused by the turning or warping of lumber or boards the result is they are no longer in the same plane. (B) A yarn term describing the number of turns per inch and direction of twist of either the singles or plies around their axes. Twist direction is either right or left handed, also called Z or S-twist. Carpet yarns usually have rather low twists, in the 2.5 to 6.0 turns per inch (TPI) range, with the majority in the 3.5 to 5.0 TPI range.

Twist carpet: Pile texture created with tightly twisted yarns in which the ply twist is substantially greater than the singles twist, causing the yarn to curl. Most twist styles are cut-pile, and the unbalanced hard twist causes a nubbly texture.

Two-tones: A design or pattern obtained by using two shades of the same colors.

U

Umbrella stand: A nineteenth century stand made from wood or marble etc.

Underframing: The supports for tables, chairs and desks.

Underglaze: The paint that is applied to porcelain before the glaze.

Underlay: See Carpet Cushion.

Underpainting: The first coat of paint applied to fine art.

Under the molding: Same as the tack down type of wall to wall installation except that the base shoe molding is replaced.

Undressed timber: Unsanded timber.

Upholstered furniture: Interior furniture covered, in whole or part, with a fabric or similar material.

Upholsterer: One who applies coverings usually of fabric to furniture.

Upholstery: Covering applied to wood furniture.

Upholstery fabric: The material used to enclose the main support system and upholstery filling af a piece of furniture.

Upholstery filling: Padding, stuffing, or filling material used in a furniture item.

Upright: A vertical post on the back of a chair.

Urea and Melamine: Plastics that are resistant to acids and chemicals. Ureas temperature performance is from 70 degrees below Fahrenheit to 170 degrees above Fahrenheit and Melamines temperature performance is from 70 degrees below Fahrenheit to 210 degrees above Fahrenheit. These plastics are hard and strong but can be broken. They won't burn but flames will cause discoloration. They are mainly used for laminated surfaces, electrical devices, table ware and buttons.

Urinal: A toilet room convenience or plumbing fixture intended for men's use, and consisting of a trapped bowl, trough, or gutter, connected with a waste or drain pipe, and arranged with a flushing device similar to that for waterclosets. By extension, the apartment in which this fixture is placed or fitted up.

Urn: A vase used for decoration made from clay or stone. It can also be used to hold plants and flowers.

V

Vaisselier: (French) Dining room shelves and cabinets.

Valance: A fabric border that is pleated and found on drapes and the bottom of couches and chairs.

Vanishing Point: In perspective, a point toward which any series of parallel lines seems to converge. The point to which all parallel lines converge. All sets of parallel lines have their own vanishing point. In perspective drawing we establish vanishing points for 1, 2 and 3 point presentation but, in fact, there are an infinite number of actual vanishing points.

Varnish: A substance made from a resinous material and dissolved in linseed oil.

Veiling Reflections: The reflections of light sources in the task which reduce the contrast between detail and background (e.g. between print and paper) thus imposing a veil and decreasing task visibility. (Veiling reflections are sometimes referred to as Reflected Glare but the latter term is properly used only when specular reflections of the light source in the task and background are so bright as to be disturbing, whereas veiling reflections are often much less obvious; their subtle effect in reducing contrast and thus visibility is nonetheless present.)

Velour: Velvet-like napped fabric with a satin or plain weave.

Velvet: Soft thick pile fabric, woven face to face on the loom and then cut apart.

Veneer: A thin sheet or layer of wood, usually rotary cut, sliced or sawn from a log or flitch. Thickness may vary from 1/100" to 1/4".

Velvet carpet: Woven carpet made on a loom similar to a Wilton loom but lacking the Jacquard motion. Velvet carpets are generally level loop or plush in solid or tweed colors.

Velvet finish: A smooth surface texture on dense plush carpet.

Velvet weave: A woven carpet type. The velvet loom first anchors the face yarns in the interwoven threads of the backing as the carpet is being made. Then, the face yarns are carried over steel wires set in the loom at predetermined heights to form loops of the yarn on the surface of the carpet. In the past these loops were cut which imparted a velvet look to the completed product and gave this weave its name. At first, velvet carpets were woven of solid colors in pile heights ranging from closely woven low pile to longer plush fabrics. Later, some carpet surfaces were made of yarns that consisted of two or more strands of different colors twisted into a single piece of yarn. These yarns, called moresque, imparted a tweedlike effect to the pile. Advanced carpet technology enables the velvet loom to produce textures other than the traditional conventional cut pile. Among these are twisted cut pile, uncut loops, combinations of cut and uncut loops, patterns in stripes or squares, as well as multilevel sculptured designs. Still another modification of the velvet loom produces carpets whose pile yarns are woven completely through the back. This type of construction is generally used in commercial areas where an increased tuft retention of the pile yarns in a carpet is desirable in order to cope with high traffic conditions.

Veneer, quartered: Veneer in which a log is sliced or sawed to bring out certain figures produced by the medullary or pith rays, which are especially conspicuous in oak. The log is flitched in several different

ways to allow the cutting of the veneer in a radial direction.

Veneer, rift cut: Veneer in which the rift or comb grain effect is obtained by cutting at an angle of about 15 degrees off of the quartered position. Twenty-five percent (25%) of the exposed surface area of each piece of veneer may contain medullary ray flake.

Veneer, rotary cut: Veneer in which the entire log is centered in a lathe and is turned against a broad cutting knife which is set into the log at a slight angle.

Veneer, sliced: Veneer in which a log or sawn flitch is held securely in a slicing machine and is thrust downward into a large knife which shears off the veneer in sheets.

Venetian glass: A fifteenth century glass that is thinly blown.

Venetian painted furniture: A style of eighteenth century furniture that was carved and painted with flowers and birds. The furniture originated from the rococo style and was developed by the Venetian family.

Vermeil: A decorative gilded metal that turns a rosy color and is used on silver or bronze.

Vermiculation: Masonry block decoration consisting of shallow channels resembling worm tracks.

Vernis Martin: An imitation Chinese lacquer that isn't very durable and attributed to the French Martin brothers.

Verrier: (French) Glassware cabinet.

Vertical access: Stairs, ramps, elevators or other means of traveling from one floor level to another. In designing access for physically handicapped people, escalators are usually not considered as an acceptable means of vertical access.

Vibration service lamps: See rough service lamps.

Victorian period: Time given Queen Victoria's reign from 1837-1901. The Victorian era is divided into three segments, early Victorian 1837-1850, middle Victorian 1850-1880, and late Victorian 1880-1901. Furniture styles started with simple carvings but later became ornate. Rosewood and mahogany wood were mainly used and were covered with damask, satin, or plush.

Vienna furniture: See bentwood furniture.

View points: The observer point and the horizon line make the major determination about the effect of the view. The further away an observer gets from the picture plane, the flatter the view gets. Also, the position of the picture plane in relationship to the view affects the image.

Vinyl: Heavy vinyl film a minimum of 4 mils in thickness, opaque or reversed printed types.

Vis-i-vis: (French) Two attached seats facing in opposite directions.

Visual Comfort Probability: (VCP) A discomfort glare calculation that predicts the percent of observers positioned at a specific location, (usually four feet in front of the center of the rear wall), who would be expected to judge a lighting condition to be comfortable. VCP rates the luminaire in its environment, taking into account such factors as illumination level, room dimensions and reflectances, luminaire type, size and light distribution, number and location of luminaries, and observer location and line of sight. The higher the VCP, the more comfortable the lighting environment. IES has established a value of 70 as the minimum acceptable VCP.

Visual edge: The line on a isolux chart which has a value equal to 10% of the maximum illumination.

Visual field: The field of view that can be perceived when the head and eyes are kept fixed.

Vitrine: (French) A glass front curio cabinet. A cabinet used to display decorative objects with a glass door.

Voile: Sheer plain-weave fabric made from highlytwisted yarn.

Volt (V): The unit for measuring electric potential. It defines the force or pressure of electricity.

W

Wainscot: A lower interior wall surface that contrasts with the wall surface above it. Unless otherwise specified, it shall be 4'-0" in height above the floor.

Wainscot chair: A sixteenth and seventeenth century armchair with a foursquare frame and panels that are attached.

Wall bracket: A shelf that rests on a wall and used to display art objects, vases, or figurines.

Wall carpet: Usually made on the tufting machine with a low one level looped pile as a light fabric. It is manufactured in a narrow width for ease of handling during its installation.

Wall covering: Any type of paper, plastic, fabric or other material fastened to a wall as a finish surface.

Walls: Vertical partitions dividing one space from another or enclosing a space. They may or may not bear a load from above.

Wall wash lighting: A smooth even distribution of light over a wall.

Walnut: A hard wood dark brown in color used almost exclusively in furniture making. This is because it receives polish well and is easy to work with.

Wane: Bark or lack of wood from any cause, except eased edges, on the edge or corner fit a piece of lumber.

Wardrobe: A sixteenth and seventeenth century cabinet used to store and hang clothes.

Warp pile: In carpet weaving, the warp yarns forming the pile. See Warp.

Wash: A thin coat of plaster, cement or paint applied to a surface or material.

Washability: The ability to withstand occasional cleaning with an appropriate detergent solution.

Wash stand: A piece of bathroom furniture that holds a soap dish and basin.

Waterfall: The term given to the covering of one or more steps tread and riser, in one continuous piece of carpet.

Waterford glass: An Irish glass ideal for cutting in deep relief. It has been manufactured since 1730.

Water repellent: A wood-treating solution which in the treating process deposits waterproof or water-resistant solids on the walls of wood fibers and ray cells, thereby retarding their absorption of water. (Noun) Having the quality of retarding the absorption of liquid water by wood fibers and ray cells. (Adjective)

Watt: (W) The unit for measuring electric power. It defines the power or energy consumed by an electrical device. The cost of operating an electrical device is determined by the watts it consumes times the hours of use. It is related to volts and amps by the following formula: Watts = Volts x Amps.

Wave molding: A molding consisting of a convex curve between two concave curves.

Webbing: Thin pieces of fabric in which spring units of furniture are attached.

Wedge technique: A method of carrying half a breadth of carpet and then placing it onto the adhesive previously spread on the floor in a glue down installation.

Weft or Woof: Yarns which run widthwise in woven cloth or carpet, interlacing with the various warp yarns. See Filling Yarn.

Weighting: Finishing materials applied to a fabric to increase its weight.

Well matched for color and grain: For the purpose of this glossary, this phrase means that the members shall be selected so that the color of adjacent members is similar and nearly uniform in appearance. The grain figure or other natural character markings shall be similar in character and appearance. Members with only flat grain shall not be permitted adjacent to members with only vertical grain. Members with mixed grain are only permitted adjacent to members with similar grain at the adjacent edge.

Welsh dresser: A seventeenth century dresser with an open shelved cabinet on top and drawers below.

Welt: A cord that is covered with fabric and sewn to the seam in upholstery. Its main purpose is for decoration.

Welt edge: The seam or border edge of a pillow, cushion, arm, or back of a piece of furniture.

Wet-dry vacuum: A tank type of vacuum cleaning machine capable of picking up liquids without damage to the machine or motor.

Wet seaming: A seaming system that uses a liquid latex adhesive and a specially made tape to join two pieces of carpet.

What-not: See etagere.

Wheel-back chair: A chair with a back that looks similar to a spoked wheel and a pierced splat for decoration.

Wicker: Flexible twigs or pieces of wood that are woven into furniture or baskets.

Width: The cross-direction wall covering measurement after trimming for hanging.

Wilton: A type of woven carpet and the loom used to manufacture it. Wilton looms have Jacquard pattern mechanisms which use punched cards to select pile height and yarn color. The carpets are often patterned or have multilevel surface. The Jacquard device raises one pre-determined pile yarn at a time to the surface leaving the remaining yarns buried in the center and back of the carpet in the warp direction.

Wilton weave: A woven carpet type. This loom weaving technique is similar to that of the Velvet loom in some respects. However, it uses perforated pattern cards similar to IBM computer cards which automatically regulate the feeding of five of six different colored yarns into the carpet. One color at a time is brought to the surface to become part of the pile. The rest are imbedded in the fabric. These buried layers of yarn serve as a cushion for the pile tufts and give added resilience and strength to the carpet. This regulating mechanism, called "Jacquard" after its inventor, permits weaving intricate patterns and many pile heights into one piece of carpet. Straight or twisted yarns can be woven at almost any level and the higher pile yarns can be cut or looped to form carved effects thus producing unlimited design opportunities. The Wilton loom, like the Velvet loom, also can weave the pile yarn completely through the back.

Window: An opening for the admission of light and sometimes of air into the interior of a building; and, by extension, the filling of this opening with glass, as usual in modern times, with the frame and sash, or casement, and their accessories. The term is usually confined to openings in vertical or nearly vertical surfaces, as walls. It is impracticable to distinguish in terms between the opening and the filling, as can be done between Doorway and Door.

Windsor chair: A chair with a high back and a saddle seat. The back can be of various designs such as, fan-back, wheel-back or loop-back.

The legs are often splayed and connected with a crossbar. It has been popular since the eighteenth century.

Wine cooler: A container that had a lead lining and held cold water or ice. It became popular in the early 1700s and was made with silver, marble, pewter or mahogany.

Wine rack: A specialized shelf or cabinet designed to hold properly aging wine in bottles.

Wing chair: An armchair with an upholstered high back and panels on either side.

Winthorp desk: A Chippendale style desk with a front that drops and a slanted top.

Wipe off rug: As the name implies, it is a loose rug placed in a strategic spot to trap traffic soil before it reaches the main carpet body. Also known as entrance rugs or step off rugs.

Wire height: In woven carpet it is the height of the pile tufts.

Wires: Parts of carpet weaving looms composed of thin metal rods or blades on which the pile tufts are formed. Round wires produce loop pile carpet, and flat wires with sharp edges produce cut-pile (plush) textures.

Woodcut: An engraved wood block often used to print a design or pattern on fabrics and wallpaper.

Wires per inch: The number of rows of pile tufts per inch as measured along the length of a woven carpet. The higher the number, then the more stitches per inch and the closer the pile rows are to each other down to the length of the carpet.

Wood failure: The area of wood fiber remaining at the glue line following completion of a shear test and expressed as a percentage of the test area.

Wood filler: An aggregate of resin and strands, shreds, or flour of wood, which is used to fill openings in wood and provide a smooth durable surface.

Wood stain: A dye used to color wood. If the wood is light colored then it must be bleached. There are several different types of stain including, water stain, varnish stain, alcohol stain and chemical stain.

Woof: The horizontal threads on a woven fabric.

Wool: Wool is a natural fiber shorn from sheep. Different breeds of sheep, and the climate in which they are raised yield varying types of wool. Some wools are long, others short. Some are fine in texture, others are coarse, still others have different degrees of luster and resilience. Because the wool of American sheep is too soft and fine for use as carpet yarn, the carpet industry imports coarse wool from Argentina, New Zealand, Pakistan, Iraq, Syria, India, The United Kingdom and other countries. In order to obtain the diversified qualities required for carpet yarns, the various imported wools are blended together after the individual batches of raw wool have been scoured and dried. Two types of yarn are produced, worsted and woolen. Worsted yarn is made up of only long wool fibers laid parallel to each other before twisting together. These yarns are more expensive and used in only a small proportion of floor coverings. Most fabrics with wool pile use woolen yarns comprised of both long and short fibers interlocked together. The yarns form a softer, bulkier, and rougher yarn than the worsted. The characteristics or wool are; good resiliency, good resistance to abrasion, good texture retention, good resistance to soil and good cleanability. Compared to worsted system or parallel spun yarns which are common to most tufted carpets, woolen yarns are soft, bulky, and hairy. Staple for woolen spinning is short, in the 3.5 to 5.5 inch range.

Work plane: The plane at which work is done, and at which illumination is specified and measured. Unless otherwise indicated, this is assumed to be a horizontal plane 30 inches above the floor.

Work: Handling marks and/or grain raising due to moisture shall not be considered a defect.

Worked: Machined or formed in any manner except surfaced four sides.

Workmanship, first class: The finest or highest class or grade of workmanship. All joints shall be tight and true. Cabinet parts shall be square, plumb, and in alignment and securely glued. The exposed surface shall be free of splits, torn or chipped surfaces, tool marks, cross sanding, gouges, dents, sand through, and other similar type defects.

Worcester china: A soft-paste porcelain manufactured since 1751 and is made with very little clay.

Workstation: Furniture and space used by employees for longer than one-half hour at a time.

Worsted yarn: Spun yarn, composed of any natural or synthetic fiber, manufactured by the worsted or parallel spinning process. Most yarns for tufted carpet are parallel spun. Staple for worsted spinning is long, often in the 6 to 8 inch range. In worsted yarns, the fibers are relatively parallel, and the yarns are relatively smooth and compact in structure.

Woven backing: A tufted carpet term for primary or secondary backing manufactured by the weaving process. Secondary backings are usually woven jute or woven polypropylene. Primary backings are usually woven (or nonwoven) polypropylene.

Woven carpets: The manufacture of tufted carpets requires a pre-fabricated backing sheet before the tufting process begins. This is not true of woven carpets. The yarns for the backing as well as the pile yarns for the surface are woven together simultaneously on the loom as the carpet is being made. Because of this method of fabrication, the backing fibers are particularly important to the tension of the pile tufts and the strength, body, and dimensional stability of the finished product. The backing fibers commonly employed are jute, kraftcord, cotton, rayon, or in most recent times, all man-made. These fibers are spun into weft yarns, warp yarns, stuffers, and chain yarns. The weft yarns are those backing yarns, also called shots or fillings, running through the width of the carpet backing. The warp yarns are those backing yarns that run lengthwise in the carpet and consist of stuffers, or additional heavy yarns woven into the backing to give the carpet added strength and weight. They are called chain yarns. These chain yarns are termed chain binder since it binds together all of the yarns used in the weaving of the carpet. The chain binder is woven in alternate fashion first over and then under the weft yarns to pull the pile yarn down and the stuffer yarns up into a tightly woven construction. All woven carpets utilize this back fabrication method. However, the face yarns are incorporated into the fabric by techniques that differ with the particular type of weave.

Wrought iron: A hard iron that softens when heated enough to be molded into desired shape. It contains less than .02% of carbon. This is of peculiar importance, beyond that of any other hammered metal work, because partly of the abundance and the hardness of iron, but more especially on account of its power of being welded and forged. The whole system of ornamental wrought-iron work, by which the buildings of the Middle Ages or the Renaissance were beautiful throughout Europe, depends upon this property, possessed by iron alone among metals, of adhering firmly one part to another when these are first heated to a certain temperature and are then hammered together. Thus when a hinge of wrought iron is to be made for a church door with deliberate decorative purpose, it is easy to terminate each strap by a series of branches, partly by cutting the strap iron itself and bending one sprig or branch away from the others, and partly by forging other slender bars and the like, which can be welded to the original stem. The difficulty with such iron work is, however, its extreme liability to rust and the consequent necessity of doing something to protect the surface. It is in this connection that gilding has become so common in the case of ironwork. Magnificent grilles of the eighteenth century and other modern imitations of equal refinement and elaboration, if of less original beauty, are commonly

gilded in great part, and this
extensive gilding often injures
greatly their general effect.

X

X-frame chair: A seventeenth century chair that has two supports, connected to the seat, in the shape of an X.

X-stretcher: A stretch that joins chair legs in the shape of an X.

Y

Yoke-back chair: A chair that has an S-shaped crossbar on the top rail.

Yard-of-ale: A seventeenth century drinking glass that has a bulb foot and a flared mouth.

Yarn: A continuous strand composed of fibers or filaments and used in tufting, weaving, and knitting to form carpet and other fabrics. Carpet yarn is often plied and may be either spun or continuous filament. A group of fibers twisted together forming one strand.

Yarn dyeing: Dyeing yarn before tufting or weaving it into carpet. The technique of dyeing yarn in a vat.

Yarn ply: The number of singles yarns ply-twisted together to form a plied yarn.

Yarn size: Same as yarn count. See Count.

Yarn weight: Same as yarn count. See count.

Yew: A soft wood pale red in color that receives a polish well and is close grained.

Z

Zebrawood: A hard wood extremely colorful and difficult to work with. It is straight grained and strangely striped.

Zonal cavity method lighting calculation: A lighting design procedure used for predetermining the relation between the number and types of lamps or luminaries, the room characteristics, and the average illuminance on the work-plane. It takes into account both direct and reflected flux.

Zwischengoldglas: A process of laminating gold between two pieces of transparent glass.

NOTES

NOTES

NOTES

NOTES